Enduring Edge

Enduring Edge

Transforming How We Think, Create and Change

Amita Shukla

Vitamita House
Bethesda, Maryland

Published by Vitamita House, a division of Vitamita LLC, Bethesda, Maryland, USA.

www.vitamita.com

The Vitamita House and Vitamita names and logos are trademarks of Vitamita LLC. For information about permissions or discounts for bulk purchases, please e-mail edge@vitamita.com.

First Edition: October 2014

Library of Congress Control Number: 2014918301

ISBN (Paperback): 978-0-9909068-1-0
ISBN (eBook): 978-0-9909068-2-7

Printed in the United States of America

With deepest gratitude for every single experience, encounter, and conversation in my life, this is dedicated to my parents, who made it all possible.

Contents

IV. Guide

V. Arrival

Author's Note

I should not talk so much about myself
if there were anybody else whom I knew as well.
—Henry David Thoreau

The thoughts, ideas, and principles in these pages emerged from extensive research and include distillations of findings from publications, articles, books, meetings, symposia, conference proceedings, formal and informal discussions, websites, and other primary and secondary sources.

While some of these sources are included under *Notes*, listing all of them there would significantly increase the length of this book. When reference is made to "research" or "studies" in a field, further details are provided at www.vitamita.com. If anything still keeps you up at night, please feel free to e-mail edge@vitamita.com.

This is a very simple story. Any resemblance to real persons, living or dead, is truly deliberate but ultimately inconsequential. Truth is, while this is my story, it is also yours. This is the story of humankind and our mysterious mind.

Prologue

I am a part of all that I have met.
—Alfred Tennyson

It is said we are made who we truly are by a few defining moments in life—flickers of deeply human experiences that leave an imprint on our hearts and make us realize, often only years later, that we were forever transformed.

It was a frigid morning, cold even by Arctic standards, as I stood in the courtyard of Malms Skola, my new school in a small island town in Finland's Archipelago Sea. The freshly plowed snow reached above my head, encircling the courtyard like fortress walls. As I waited for my teacher to arrive, I was quickly surrounded by curious Finnish schoolchildren, who followed my every move.

Most of them were looking at a non-Scandinavian for the first time, and they examined my black hair and brown skin with a sense of cautious wonder. My parents, as young, newly married graduate students, had moved from India to

Germany to pursue their advanced studies. I was born in Kiel, a small university town on the Baltic Sea and our home for my first nine years. When I was in the fourth grade, we moved to Finland.

I helplessly looked around and longingly remembered my friends in Germany. I wanted to move my lips and say something, but no one here would understand me. I spoke only German and broken English, and they only Finnish and Swedish. As I glanced at the faces around me, a small girl with long brown hair, holding a small red dictionary, approached me.

"I, you talk English," she said, as she opened her tattered book. She proceeded to say a word in Finnish and then looked for it in the half-torn pages of the dictionary.

"Ra-aa-b-ee-t?" she asked, carefully pronouncing the word and scanning my face for a sign of approval.

"Rab-bit," I said. "You say 'rabbit.'"

She flipped through the pages again. "*Lintu*," she said. "*Lintu*. Bee-rd? Be-rrd?"

Again I tried to guess. "Bird?" I asked, flapping my arms. She nodded with excitement.

By now, the other children wondered what in her hands had brought a smile to my face. I had the English vocabulary of a toddler, but that frigid morning, surrounded by curious Finnish schoolchildren, I could have been Shakespeare, for all they knew.

Over my next six months at Malms Skola, other than a part-time interpreter the principal hired for me, no one spoke German or English. Our teacher would give instructions to my classmates and then walk over to my desk and use an amusing spectrum of Charlie Chaplin–like gestures to direct me. Laughter was our only common language. Yet with my new friends, more often than not, it was enough. During those days, on many of which I could not exchange a word with anyone, I was both in the midst of life and, in parallel, just an observer of it. Years later I realized that, deprived of meaningful speech, I quietly absorbed what remained when words held no meaning. When we are deprived of language, we are also stripped of its limitations—its labels, nuances, judgments, and constraints. We are left just being human.

~

Twenty-five years later, in the depths of winter, I stood on an MIT street corner in Cambridge, Massachusetts, waiting for a taxi after a work meeting. As plows burrowed through snow-swelled streets, students and scientists scurried between Kendall Square's labs and cafés. The muffling silence of incessant snowflakes swept me back to the Arctic days of my childhood and I began to look anew at a place I had visited countless times before.

The blocks surrounding Kendall Square, littered with redbrick warehouses during my college days, had transformed into the biomedical innovation capital of the world. Now teeming with gleaming structures that held rare promises of cures—and their even rarer realization—the rising skyline housed world-class research centers and trailblazing biotechnology companies.

I had become a principal at one of the world's largest venture capital firms, and it was my daily job to find, evaluate, and invest in healthcare innovations with the greatest potential for conquering our worst ills: cancer, heart disease, diabetes, and depression, among others. Working alongside brilliant inventors and passionate entrepreneurs, we created startups, built companies, and rode the hope-fueled journeys of promising therapies from lab benches to patients' bedsides or, when they failed, to the graveyards of fallen drugs.

That morning I had been talking to Harvard doctors and MIT scientists about their latest discoveries: newly identified biochemical pathways, revolutionary computational technologies, and novel drugs on the cusp of leaving their labs for further development. One scientist had decoded the function of a new peptide in diabetes, another the roles of neurotransmitters in depression. What nature has encoded meticulously over millennia of millennia, we yearn to decipher in our brief lifetimes. Yet it would still take more than a decade and cost hundreds of millions of dollars to transform these petri-dish inventions into real therapies for patients.

Pondering peptides and their pathways, which speak a complex language all their own, I thought about what motivates us to invest decades, fortunes, and careers into quests to discern the nuances of a single protein, pathway, or cell— all the while knowing that the journey will be filled with much more failure than success.

Shedding the language of statistics and science, I realized that the lessons of the lab bench, the startup boardroom, and the patient bedside echoed those of my childhood in Finland: we are fundamentally the same inside. Just like our hearts, our cells speak a universal language.

And while we strive to decipher how our bodies work in sickness and health, we long even more to know who we really are, why we are as we are, and how we can be our best selves. And this quest goes much deeper than even science reveals.

Maintaining and regaining health is, at heart, a desire to transform ourselves from dis-ease to ease, from where we are to where we would like to be. And health is much more than passing a physical exam at a doctor's office. True well-being comes from a deeper place. Beyond the absence of disease, it is an aspiration to not just survive but thrive—to live at our highest potential. Once our basic needs for survival—water, food, and shelter—are met, this quest leads us on a distinctly human mission: to seek meaning in our lives and create lives of meaning. We want to attain contentment and peace, to experience belonging and connection, and to be able to give our best to the world. We want to matter.

∼

Five years later, at the crack of dawn on a beautiful spring day in Northern California, I was sitting completely still, barely aware of my breath, and thinking about absolutely nothing. As time slowed to a crawl, the inner quiet took me back to the stillness of falling snow. Then, as if out of nowhere, powerful and profound insights began to dance through and descend on my mind like snowflakes—uniquely beautiful on their own but truly majestic as they blanketed the earth together.

Within a few minutes, I heard the six-thirty morning bell. With each gentle *ting-ting*, it brought me back to the wooden floor beneath my long-asleep legs, rays of sunlight dancing through the windows, and a symphony of birds, crickets, and frogs in full performance in the Sierra Nevada foothills. I was in the midst of an intensive monthlong yoga teacher-training program. For 30 days straight, from six in the morning to ten at night, in a place disconnected from civilization both physically and digitally, I studied and experienced the science, art, and mysteries of the human body, mind, and inner being.

While years of formal education and professional training had given me the knowledge and tools for navigating life, the teachings presented here, whose origins reached back millennia, suggested that the starting point for understanding and improving ourselves, and even our communities and the world, is often much simpler than we realize. And it rests in a place that is both the easiest and the hardest to access: our mind.

Yet while our world is filled with systems and tools to fill and train the mind, where do we go to learn how to *use* it better? Over the next two years, after close to nine years at the frontiers of healthcare innovation, I embarked on a journey to study the mysterious powers of the mind—through the reports of modern neuroscience and the repositories of wisdom spanning centuries.

In the silence of that California dawn, I experienced a state of mind whose glimmers I had sensed in that Finnish schoolyard and on that MIT street corner. Each time— in a flash—my perspective shifted, whirling thoughts fell into place, and wisdom emerged from within. As Malms Skola and Kendall Square waltzed through my mind, I realized that when words held no meaning, our hearts could convey what even words could not say. And when science reached its limits, our experiences could illuminate what even science could not elucidate. Also, during years of work with brilliant minds, I had observed that the most creative ones often functioned at a different level. And among entrepreneurs straddling the razor-thin line between failure and success, or sometimes even patients the one between sickness and health, I noticed that their states of mind appeared to influence outcomes. Even while evaluating investments and grappling with the limits of data, I observed that my final decisions often emerged from a deeper state of mind. I began to wonder, *what is so unique about these states of mind?*

This journey took me far and wide and ultimately deep inside. Distillations of patterns weaving in and out of humanity's knowledge and experience through the ages revealed that while the ways of the mind may seem mysterious, they are not a mystery. And they tell a universal story that weaves through centuries of human thought.

Over time, I experienced how the simple act of more deeply understanding the mind can transform how we use it. After years of searching for the most promising ideas to improve human health, I began to wonder if one of the most powerful ones might not have been with me all along. And it seemed to hold secrets not just for our well-being but also for attaining our highest potential.

~

This book is about unlocking the powers of *your* mind. We use our mind in limited ways—we think it exists just to think, but it can do so much more than that. Beyond the state of mind you are using to read these words, we will explore its other dimensions—some of which we scarcely fathom and rarely access. When we better understand our mind, we can improve how we make decisions, how we create and innovate, and how we navigate and lead change in our lives, our work, and our world. How does such a journey of transformation begin? That is the story to come.

I. Departure

CHAPTER ONE

Starting Point

Whatsoever is, is but as it were
the seed of that which shall be.
—Marcus Aurelius

Transformation is the most universal human experience. From our first breath to our last, biology continuously changes us. And from the Stone Age to the Silicon Age, humanity has led a succession of continuous transformations toward progress. Yet whether it happens to us or is initiated by us, learning how to survive and thrive through change remains a universal human challenge.

After living in Finland for less than a year, my family moved back to India. Three years later, a few days shy of my 14th birthday, we immigrated to America. When we arrived, we had few resources and no support structure. Yet while our pockets were empty, our hearts brimmed with hope. For us America was synonymous with unbounded opportunity and my parents' idealistic words resonated in my mind night and day: *The only limits imposed on you are those of your imagination, and the only resources you will be denied are those you don't seek out.* In the years that followed, I witnessed how being in the right place could change a life—not just the right physical place but, more important, the right mental place.

I spoke broken English when we arrived and received a C grade on my first essay in high school. Seven years later, I was a senior editor at the *Harvard Crimson*, my college's daily newspaper. My parents were scrappy, bootstrapping scientist-entrepreneurs and created their startup with credit card debt. Less than a decade later, they sold it and sent their daughter to the epicenter of entrepreneurship—Stanford's business school. In high school, I did a science fair project on the benefits of an Indian herb for treating gum disease. A decade later, my daily job was to find and help invest millions in groundbreaking medical treatments.

This is not just my story; it is simply the one I know best. This is also the story of countless people around the world who conquered obstacles, defied the odds, hitched their wildest dreams to slivers of hope, and transformed them into reality. These voyages are not always across oceans—they can be from poverty to wealth, sickness to health, stagnation to innovation, and failure to success. Often they are voyages of confronting our greatest fears, finding our deepest passions, or shifting from being led by our weaknesses to leading with our strengths.

The story they tell is one hidden within them, a more universal one, of what leads us from where we are to where we would like to be—the story of human transformation. To understand it better, let's begin at the most universal starting point: the human body.

How Change Begins

Our body's transitions between sickness and health are the most primal transformations we each experience in our lifetime. During my years in the trenches of healthcare innovation, as I walked through research labs and studied patient data, more fundamental questions often swirled through my mind: Why do we get sick in the first place? What is the true source of healing? How can we not just treat but cure or, better yet, prevent?

When we become ill, sometimes we recover just by giving the body some rest. In more serious situations, medical intervention can save us. Advanced surgeries and drugs, combined with significant strides in public health, have transformed many crippling and fatal maladies into curable and chronic conditions. We live in the best of times of human health and there is no doubt that the most exciting years of biomedical innovation lie ahead of us.

At the same time, looking beyond the leading edge of the cutting edge, I observed that for many of our most prevalent plagues, particularly lifestyle-driven chronic diseases, we have few breakthrough treatments on the horizon and even fewer promises of cures. This is explained partly by the complexities of diseases themselves and partly by the fact that drug design and development are reverse engineering–based processes. Scientists study the intricate biochemical pathways of proteins and enzymes that control functions such as regulating blood sugar or blood pressure. When disease disrupts these signaling cascades, we design novel molecules targeted at damaged pathways, in attempts to restore their function.

If we consider the workings of the human body like the live performance of a Beethoven symphony, we can now identify not just the instruments being played but also the faces of some of the performers. Sometimes we can tell if the first violinist is smiling, even if fleetingly. Yet the body's orchestration of signaling cascades is much more complex than a musical performance. It is also infinitely more exquisite. Even cutting-edge science is in its infancy when it comes to grasping the full notes of a symphony, learning which violin plays a specific part and when a performance starts and ends.

Our latest tools can open a heart vessel, screw together a broken bone, or remove a tumor, but healing itself is still largely a mystery. For many diseases, so are their initiation, intensity, and relapse. By the time a condition is diagnosed, the body has often been on a degenerative path for years (sometimes decades). Many drugs for chronic diseases address their symptoms or slow their progression yet fail to treat their true origins. Patients often become dependent on such drugs for life and, in exchange for relief of their symptoms, endure drug side effects.

This problem is not just a small part of healthcare—it is most of it. Chronic diseases account for the majority of close to $3 trillion in annual US healthcare expenditures.[1] About half of all adult Americans suffer from at least one chronic condition, and 7 of the top 10 causes of death are chronic diseases such as heart disease, stroke, cancer, diabetes, and obesity.[2]

In addition, the National Institute of Mental Health (NIMH), of the National Institutes of Health (NIH), estimates that about 20 percent of adult Americans are afflicted by any mental illness in a given year, with anxiety and mood disorders, such as depression, leading the pack.[3] Close to 520 million US prescriptions for mental health drugs were written in 2013, with total spending nearing $24 billion.[4]

Chronic diseases are also growing at epidemic rates in industrializing nations such as India and China. The World Health Organization (WHO) pegs depression as the "leading cause of disability worldwide," affecting more than "350 million people of all ages" and significantly contributing to the world's 1 million annual suicides.[5] This tragic waste of life equals 2,500 jetliners, each with 400 people aboard, crashing with no survivors—all due to preventable self-inflicted harm.

∾

A closer look at how we approach chronic conditions offers instructive insights into transformation—for our health *and* our lives. Consider this simple analogy: A kitchen faucet has been left running, and after a while, the sink starts overflowing. Cleaners come in with mops to get the water off the floor. Drugs are external solutions, like mops. As the water keeps flowing, more mops are needed, and if flooding continues, the cleaners will eventually be overwhelmed.

Similarly, in our body, when the "faucet" of disease runs unabated, the effectiveness of many drugs declines over time. Many of the body's functions have redundancies, and when one malfunctions, others try to compensate. Yet even our body's best efforts are limited if we disregard its warning signs. Once the body breaks down, we come to appreciate its functions most acutely. Out-of-control blood sugar or spiking blood pressure poses immediate risks to several organs. Once a house floods, all possible approaches are needed to remove the water. With survival at stake, drugs are often the best solution. Yet in the long run, when we maintain our focus on inventing better mops, we neglect finding ways to turn off the faucet.

In the early stages of disease, the body's warning signs are easier to ignore. We may hear water dripping, but it poses no immediate danger, and even when some spills, mops can take care of it. A drug often "permits" us to maintain the lifestyle that made us sick in the first place, and we become dependent on it for managing disease. Pills and procedures play an important part, but we can prevent and cure more often than we do—much more.

The faucet represents the root cause of a challenge. When examined through their root causes, many chronic diseases appear to have a simple starting point for conquest. Just as a headache can be a symptom of migraine, a migraine can be a symptom of deeper physical distress, which can often be traced to mental stress. Under stress, each body responds differently: some develop migraines, others diabetes, weight gain, high blood pressure, addictions, mental disorders, a weakened immune system, or even certain allergies. In a state of stress, the cure lies not just in treating the reactions in our body but also in examining the state of our mind.

In addition, in healthcare, it is well established that while access to care and genetic, social, and environmental factors are important determinants of health, lifestyle plays a major role in preventing many chronic conditions such as heart disease, diabetes, obesity, high blood pressure, and depression. A 2014 WHO study reports that even half of all cancers can be prevented with application of our current knowledge and implementation of changes in diet, exercise, and alcohol and tobacco use.[6]

Yet despite our knowing that the greatest contributors to the personal, societal, and economic costs of healthcare are within our actionable control, why do they persist? What prevents us from solving problems for which we already have solutions? Why, despite knowing what is good for us, do we still not do it? Even when we initiate small personal changes, such as losing weight, reducing stress, eating healthier foods, and balancing our time, we often fall short of our goals—not to mention the struggles we face in dealing with more drastic changes, such as disease diagnoses, career setbacks, or relationship failures. Why is change so difficult?

Examples of transformation failure are all around us. Business schools are rich repositories of case studies on companies and brands (e.g., Borders, Polaroid, Blockbuster) that struggled with change, failed to transform, and perished. Several American cities, once thriving centers of commerce (e.g., Baltimore, Detroit), have struggled with reinvention as their bedrock industries have declined or disappeared.

Even in the public policy arena, many initiatives and laws designed to address our greatest challenges—in health, education, poverty, and the environment—fall short of attaining their desired goals. Our approaches often hold a de facto assumption that it is too difficult to transform ourselves and thus we design policies that are supposed to work despite how we operate.

We create complex carrots and sticks, incentives and penalties to encourage certain behaviors and discourage others. Yet, this is akin to designing drugs to alleviate the symptoms of diseases, rather than finding and treating their root causes. When we start downstream from the source of a problem, we often fall short. At that level, complexity pervades and our solutions address short-term or surface-level aspects of it. Change can be temporary, resistance high, and failure prevalent.

Many times, the problems for which we develop complex, cutting-edge solutions have simple and more effective alternatives. Sometimes the solutions are so simple, we overlook them. Or our biases lead us to dismiss them, especially when they fail to fit into our preset ways of looking at the world. At their origins, often traceable to a single starting point, challenges reveal their simplest essence. Once a problem becomes simpler, so does developing solutions.

For many challenges, we can turn off, or at least turn down, the faucet much more often and more easily than we realize. Over the long run, turning a faucet requires less effort and fewer resources than mobilizing mops. It enables downstream ripple effects and is often the only real solution. As we shift our attention to faucets, we arrive at the true starting point for transformation. Then change is lasting, acceptance higher, and failure temporary.

Where Change Begins

As I embarked on this journey, the more deeply I examined change, the more I was convinced that inner transformation does not happen to us—it begins within us. The change we seek on the outside often starts with a few kernels of change inside. My research and explorations across diverse fields kept guiding me back to the same single starting point for transformation. The true faucet of change is in our mind, but not just within it—it is the mind itself.

Although we use it every moment of our lives and it most defines our time on Earth, our mind is the part of us we understand the least. It doesn't come with a user's manual, although we desperately wish it did, because often, despite all our intelligence, our mind perplexes us—and sometimes its capacity astounds us.

The truth is, our mind can do much more than we do with it. We learn about its powers in sporadic ways that even geniuses across fields struggle to explain. Doctors speak of miraculous healing, inventors and scientists of remarkable insights, artists and writers of mysterious muses, and leaders of brilliant acumen, all guiding humanity's most marvelous moments.

In fact, most stories of human revolution, repair, resurrection, and reincarnation through the ages can be traced to individuals who unlocked and unleashed the powers of their mind. Among greats throughout history—and those who walked the earth more recently, such as Mother Teresa, Nelson Mandela, Mahatma Gandhi, and Martin Luther King Jr.—most traced the beginnings of their worldly work to extraordinary inner transformation. Change started within them, rippled into their societies, and ultimately transformed humanity.

We spend our lives acquiring skills, performing tasks, and absorbing information, yet inner transformation is not part of any résumé, promotion, or awards ceremony. Nonetheless, whether our cause is transforming society or conquering a personal weakness, our success depends on it. So how do we learn to make the most of our mind?

In recent decades, science has intensified its study of the mind as new technologies have made leaps in our ability to study the brain. But many dimensions of our mind remain beyond measurement even with our most sophisticated tools. While we can measure the beat of our heart, the pressure in our vessels, and the biochemistry of our blood, how do we measure the state of our mind?

We often write off the mysterious dimensions of our mind as inexplicable, or we think of insights as random occurrences—moments when complexities dissolve, dilemmas resolve, and answers emerge. Yet within each of us are vast reservoirs of wisdom and insights to address our most vexing challenges. If we can figure out how to harness them, we can unlock tremendous human potential.

During this journey, when science reached its limits, I explored the mind through the lens of other fields. I discovered deep wisdom in philosophy, religion, art, and healing traditions, which have been students of the mind for millennia. I also gleaned insights from the many journeys of transformation I witnessed over the years: patients finding health, innovators expressing creativity, and entrepreneurs attaining success. Over time, I realized that the potential to transform how we use our mind rests not in a few "gifted" minds but in how we each use our own. The power to attain our highest potential is within each of us.

Why Change?

Knowing how to use our mind more effectively is a skill we need more urgently today than ever. No generation before ours has faced as direct a threat to the traditional functions of the mind. From the advent of humanity until a few centuries ago, most human activity was physical labor. Starting with the industrial revolution, we developed machines with physical capabilities vastly exceeding our muscular capacities. We transitioned from being the machine to becoming its operator. Now, ever-more-powerful computers in our offices, homes, and pockets are surpassing and supplanting human mental data storage and processing capabilities. Today an education, even one in specific skills, no longer guarantees a lifelong career. Just as typists have vanished with their typewriters, many more jobs will face extinction in the years to come.

Industries such as medicine, law, and publishing are confronting dramatic disruption. An idea that could serve as the decades-long foundation for a company can now be commoditized in a fraction of that time. Exponential improvements in machine learning and artificial intelligence create the potential to replace even higher-level functions of our mind, such as driving cars, recognizing patterns in complexity, making medical diagnoses, and writing reports. As machines increasingly replace the work of both our bodies and our minds, we are forced to confront the ultimate question: What is the enduring role of humans? And how do we best use our mind to thrive in the future?

In the years to come, our "intelligence" will be defined, more than ever, by our ability to mentally adapt and advance in rapidly evolving ecosystems. In a world flattened by technology, our enduring edge will be not only what we put into our mind but also how we use it.

Furthermore, technology creates unprecedented opportunities to unlock our highest potential. Freed of more mundane and repetitive tasks, such as data computation and recall, we can direct our mind's attention to its most powerful and uniquely human functions: unleashing our creative and innovative potential, promoting healing and well-being, and developing lasting solutions in fields from education to the environment. We can focus more on nurturing meaning, compassion, and contentment in our communities and help each other realize our full potential, individually and collectively.

Humanity's future progress will be led by minds that can extract not only knowledge from data but also wisdom from knowledge. A mind grounded in rote memorization can be driven to obsolescence much more swiftly than one with mastery of creativity, adaptability, and perseverance. An expert yoked to proprietary information risks becoming outmoded much more easily than one who can create links between disparate fields and generate novel solutions. A leader operating through fear faces higher threats to survival than one comfortable navigating ambiguity and leading with authenticity.

Even in the world's most advanced nations, the progress that remains to be made is unleashing the potential of all—not just a few, but all—minds. It will determine the difference between those who lead and those who lag in the future. And this holds true for nations and organizations as much as for each of us. The sooner we master our mind, the more we can use its powers in our lifetime to conquer challenges and realize dreams. This is the most critical skill we need to teach our children. Because, those who learn to harness the powers of their mind do more than transform their lives—they change the world.

Before We Begin

Our time in this world is limited. None of us knows exactly how much we have left. Your time with these pages is more fleeting still—a few hours, if you are not distracted sooner. Still, as you travel through them, bring your mind to them— not a small, distracted part, but your complete attention. You may be thinking, *I have no time!* This will not consume your time. In fact, you will gain time. Clarity of mind brings lucidity to life. We can do more with less. Much more.

As we embark on this journey into the mind, we start the way my own began, with insights on the mind from medicine, science, and human wisdom through the ages (Chapter 2). Then the adventure continues as we obtain a simple map to explore the different terrains of our mind (Chapters 3–6). Next we gain a powerful compass to help navigate our travels (Chapters 7–10). Then we attain a travel guide with practical signposts to show us the way (Chapters 11–12). And, finally, we begin creating paths toward new adventures in our own lives (Chapters 13–15).

Before we begin, please remember that these words that speak to you are just the journey of one mind. Yet the ideas within them can guide any mind—like a map or compass that aids all travelers. Your terrain is your own mind, with its own unique experiences, thoughts, and aspirations. Within it, you will discover your own paths and journeys. Also, the principles presented here apply as much to companies, organizations, and even nations, as they do to individual lives. For, regardless of the configurations in which we organize our 7 billion, all our entities, structures, and systems are comprised of the same essential building blocks: humans.

Also, while this book emerged from insights and patterns gathered from extensive research, it is not intended to be a systematic, exhaustively referenced publication. It is a distillation of my observations, like a casual conversation—what we might talk about during a leisurely dinner or over coffee on a relaxing Sunday afternoon.

This journey changed my life, which is what has brought me to you, here, now. I am sharing this story with the simple hope that if a few of its words help just one other mind, which may then guide another, perhaps, mind by mind, we can transform the world together.

CHAPTER TWO

Turning Point

What we observe is not nature in itself but
nature exposed to our method of questioning.
—Werner Heisenberg

One winter early in my venture capital career, I was
flying over the serene, snow-capped peaks of America's
heartland to a bustling biotechnology conference in San
Francisco. Sitting next to me was a friendly, grandfatherly
gentleman. We chatted about childhoods, career paths, and
creativity. The arc of his life spanned over seven decades and
that of his impact many more. With the perspective of his
years, he offered a few words of advice.

"Whatever you want in life, imagine it in such exquisite
detail that it feels real to you; make it so tangible that you
believe you have it already," he said. With a twinkle in his
eye, he encouraged me to visualize what I would see and
feel, what I would be thinking, and what each of my senses
would experience. I realized he was guiding me to explore
the powers of my mind.

He should know, I thought. After immigrating to America as a child, he not only grew up to make landmark discoveries in physics, but also was bestowed with its highest honor—the Nobel Prize. In the years to come, in subtle yet remarkable ways, I discovered the power of his wisdom in the most unlikely places.

Trials and Tribulations

The glittering ballroom at one of the most famous hotels in Washington, DC, a few blocks from the White House, was an ocean brimming with dark suits. Biotechnology leaders from around the country had gathered on this early-spring day in 2005 to learn about new therapies for devastating diseases such as cancer and diabetes, and for seemingly epidemic afflictions such as pain, insomnia, addiction, and attention deficit hyperactivity disorder (ADHD).

The conference consisted of long days filled with back-to-back, rapid-fire presentations by biotech executives on the latest drugs being developed by their companies. These were the crème de la crème of biomedical breakthroughs, yet among the hundreds presented here, just a few would survive the grueling clinical-trial process required to demonstrate safety and effectiveness in patients.

Investors in the audience aspired to predict the winners. Such investment decisions are based on evaluating imperfect information and trying to forecast a world that does not yet exist: How will we be treating this disease in a decade, when the drug under investigation is expected to reach patients—assuming success? How do we know if a drug that shrinks tumors in mice will do the same in humans? How do we determine if a drug effective in carefully controlled trials with a few dozen patients will have the same effect in a broader patient population?

I tried to analyze which of the treatments presented at this conference promised the greatest potential of benefit to patients *and* held the highest chance of surviving the high-risk validation process. The stakes were high. Investments in a company spanned from tens of millions to hundreds of millions of dollars. If a drug failed during trials, there might be nothing of value left. And a decision to fund a new therapy was often literally a matter of life and death—either helping a new drug become a beacon of hope for patients who often had no other, or leaving it to languish in lab rats and test tubes, sometimes forever.

Among the thousands of presentations I saw during my close to nine years in this role, one in particular—presented at this conference—captivated me, as much for the results it showed as for the story it told.

Before a new drug can be prescribed to patients, it has to be approved by the US government's Food and Drug Administration (FDA). Before the FDA took shape and implemented regulatory standards in 1962, the United States had a rampant and thriving "snake oil" industry. Early 20th-century newspapers are filled with advertisements for potions and elixirs that claimed to cure many of the same maladies from which we still suffer today. Most had no proof of benefit. Many contained cocaine, heavy metals, such as lead, mercury, and arsenic, and other ingredients that caused significant harm, as illustrated by the articles on quackery, poisonings, and deaths sprinkled through the same newspapers.

The FDA process of proving that a drug's benefits outweigh its harms begins in test tubes and animals. For instance, obesity is studied in mice fed high-fat diets and asthma in rabbits that have inhaled a lung irritant. Cancers are often studied by growing human tumor cells in mice. Such experiments avoid prematurely risking the lives of humans, because many drugs are potent poisons too. The difference between healing and harming (or killing) is often just a matter of dose.

During the next round of tests, clinical trials in humans, investors commit significant capital to fund further development. After each round of trials, results are shared at meetings such as the one I attended in Washington, DC. The study that captured my attention there was a phase III trial. While early studies, known as phase I and II clinical trials, provide data from small groups of patients, the gold standard of evidence for FDA approval of a therapy consists of placebo-controlled, randomized, double-blind, multicenter phase III trials, defined as follows:

1. *Placebo-controlled*: A placebo is a harmless sugar or "fake" pill that contains no active ingredients yet is designed to appear identical to the drug. A subset of phase III patients receives a placebo, instead of the drug.
2. *Randomized*: Patients are randomly assigned to receive either the drug or the placebo. All patients also receive the existing standard of care, ensuring adequate medical support.
3. *Double-blind*: Neither the doctors and nurses conducting the study nor the enrolled patients know if they are getting the drug or the placebo. Both are "blind."

4. *Multicenter*: The trial is conducted in hundreds or thousands of patients across diverse centers intended to reflect "real-world" variability in treatment practices and patient demographics.

The phase III trial that caught my attention was for an injectable drug to treat alcohol dependence, a condition that exacts a heavy toll. According to the WHO, more than 3 million global deaths can be attributed to alcohol each year, as can more than 200 different health conditions, including liver diseases and cancers.[7] In addition, alcohol is a major contributor to driving fatalities, domestic violence, and violent crime. Its underlying cause, addiction, encompasses dependence on, and abuse of, a much broader spectrum of substances (e.g., opioid painkillers) and activities (e.g., gambling) and is responsible for even greater personal and societal harm.

The 627 patients enrolled in this six-month phase III trial were randomized into three groups, each receiving a monthly injection of high-dose drug, low-dose drug, or placebo. All received standardized, low-intensity psychosocial support. As the trial results were projected on the vast ballroom screen, one chart, in particular, became etched onto my mind.

At the start of the trial, the enrolled patients had a median of about 19–20 heavy drinking days (HDDs) per month. A HDD represents the consumption of at least five standard drinks for a man and four standard drinks for a woman.[8] A standard drink contains 0.6 ounces of pure alcohol and equals about 12 ounces of beer, 5 ounces of wine, or 1.5 ounces of hard liquor.[9]

At the end of the six-month study, patients in the low-dose drug group had about 25 percent fewer HDDs relative to patients on placebo. And patients in the high-dose drug group had about 50 percent fewer HDDs relative to patients on placebo. Such reductions in HDDs seemed impressive.

But here was the astonishing fact: the median HDDs per month for the placebo group itself were about 6 days by the end of the study, down from 19–20 days at the start. Thus, patients who received no drug experienced an astounding reduction in HDDs of nearly 70 percent! The incremental decrease from about 6 days in the placebo group to about 4.5 HDDs in the low-dose group (a 25 percent relative reduction) and about 3 HDDs in the high-dose group (a 50 percent relative reduction) amounted to about 1.5 and 3 days per month, respectively.

Beyond the data, whose nuances experts dissect with surgical attention to detail, I was most captivated by the principle behind them: Placebo patients receiving standard care and no drug saw significant improvement in their condition. This phenomenon, treatment benefit in the absence of "active" drugs, is known as the placebo effect and it is pervasive in drug development.

∽

The placebo effect has been reported in clinical trials spanning a range of medical conditions, including pain, migraine, depression, anxiety, asthma, gastrointestinal disorders, and sexual dysfunction. It has even been seen in "sham" surgeries for knee and back pain, in which placebo patients receiving a superficial incision, instead of deeper surgical treatment of their joint or spine, report an improvement in their underlying condition. Even when patients know they are receiving a placebo, positive expectations can generate the placebo effect.

A study published in 2010 by Ted Kaptchuk, a Harvard professor and placebo expert, showed that in 80 patients with irritable bowel syndrome, the placebo effect could be harnessed by providing them with "1) an accurate description of what is known about placebo effects, 2) encouragement to suspend disbelief, 3) instructions that foster a positive but realistic expectancy, and 4) directions to adhere to the medical ritual of pill taking."[10]

The placebo effect has been among the leading causes of phase III trial failure in recent decades and has drowned billions of dollars in drug development. Placebos often "work," and, much to the chagrin of drug developers, their net effects can exceed those of drugs, because placebos have no harmful side effects. While drug developers consider the placebo effect a major nuisance, and an expensive one at that, the more I looked into it, the more it intrigued me.

I remembered the wise physicist's words on the power of visualizing a desired future. A strong placebo effect suggests that patients' imagining they are receiving a drug can sometimes be as effective as their taking it. Or even in the absence of placebo pills, when patients expect their condition will improve, it often does.

Science is befuddled by unexplainable healing and uncertain how to evaluate it. Yet for the patient who experiences it, it is as real as a treatment. And whether it is a placebo effect or a "therapeutic" effect becomes a matter of semantics, because the placebo is therapeutic.

The powerful effects of our mind on our body are further validated by the opposite of the placebo effect—the nocebo effect. Nocebo means that negative expectations can harm our health. In clinical trials, when patients are told they may experience a drug's side effects, such as headaches, dizziness, nausea, or pain, they often start experiencing them even when receiving only a placebo.

Thus, negative thoughts and anticipation, such as worry, anxiety, fear, and stress, can make us feel and become sick. Studies indicate that patients affected by the nocebo effect can have reduced immunity, slowed healing, increased pain, and other symptoms instigated by the mind.

In essence, clinical trials, albeit unintentionally, demonstrate how our mind can make us feel better—and worse. We can take this a step further to consider that in any disease with a significant placebo effect in clinical trials, the mind likely influences healing.

Medicine struggles with how best to apply this concept while treating patients. Doctors would risk malpractice if they prescribed sugar pills instead of drugs. Some draw upon the placebo effect's power by choosing positive words that encourage and elicit positive expectations in patients while still accurately conveying health information. In doing so, they meld the science of medicine with the art of healing, becoming doctors to the body and healers to the mind.

Yet while medicine may be limited in how it applies the placebo effect, we can each use this free and powerful force on ourselves to supplement our well-being anytime. We need not be "blind" to it or worry about side effects, since it has no risk of overdose. Moreover, we can use it not just when we are sick but also when we are healthy, because its powers extend far beyond healing our body. How can we experience this? By becoming aware of how our mind affects us, as these brief thought experiments illustrate:

1. Imagine holding a bright green lime and then cutting it in half with a knife. Now imagine smelling the citrus scent released by the fresh-cut surface and then bringing your tongue to it to lick it. At this moment, you might notice increased saliva in your mouth. We can generate physical responses to thoughts of stimuli as if they are real. Different expectations of pleasure or displeasure create varied physical responses.

2. Now, think of a person you love and imagine that person sharing his or her greatest joy with you. We tend to get washed over with feelings of warmth when we imagine this. The body's biochemistry can change with such a response and release hormones and neurotransmitters that make us feel good within.

3. Next, think of someone who irritates you so much that you avoid him or her. Now imagine that person invading your space. Just this much thinking can induce shallow breathing, tense muscles, and increased blood pressure and stress hormone levels. This negative response creates sensations of resistance and harms us within.

These simple exercises and the placebo and nocebo effects offer proof of how our thoughts can change our body. Intrigued, I ventured next into the powerhouse of thought, our most complex and mysterious organ—the brain.

Science of Change

In the late fall of 2005, six months after the biotechnology conference, another gathering of innovation pioneers took place in Washington, DC. This one literally represented the world's brain trust as close to 35,000 doctors and scientists gathered to share their latest brain research findings at the annual meeting of the Society for Neuroscience (SfN).

For the first time in its history, the SfN decided to invite a most unlikely speaker to deliver one of its keynote lectures. This man was neither a scientist nor a doctor. He was neither the author of any breakthrough publications in this field nor one who treated patients in the traditional sense. He was also not a patient, although in recent years neuroscientists had developed a keen interest in minds like his.

His primary "credential" was having been a student and master of our being in both body and mind—work he had been pursuing for more than seven decades. He spoke broken English, yet his words flawlessly conveyed deep understanding of our most human essence.

The speaker was the Dalai Lama, a man considered the modern leader of the Buddhist faith, although his insights on humanity have led many to rank him among the greatest minds of our times. Humble, charming, and disarmingly humorous, he had traveled halfway around the world with the eagerness of a curious child to converse with the world's brightest minds about its workings.

At another meeting preceding his SfN lecture, he had spent hours engaged in lively discussions, peppering neuroscientists with penetrating questions about their latest research findings.

On the day of his talk at the SfN annual meeting, the Dalai Lama published an editorial in the *New York Times* distilling his planned remarks. He described a childhood experience of using a telescope to look at the moon, during which he was surprised to learn that the moon is a rock with craters, and not a glowing source of light, as fourth-century cosmology texts had taught him.

He wrote, "If science proves some belief of Buddhism wrong, then Buddhism will have to change. In my view, science and Buddhism share a search for the truth and for understanding reality. By learning from science about aspects of reality where its understanding may be more advanced, I believe that Buddhism enriches its own worldview."[11]

The Dalai Lama recognized that when we look at the world through one lens—or even just the lenses we view as representing our truths—we limit our capacity to access holistic knowledge essential for human progress. His editorial continued by describing recent neuroscience research on Buddhist monks engaged in extensive concentration and cessation of thought, practices commonly referred to as meditation. These studies suggested that meditation could decrease activity in parts of the brain associated with negative stress responses and increase it in those linked to happiness, peacefulness, and compassion. The Dalai Lama continued, "If practices from my own tradition can be brought together with scientific methods, then we may be able to take another small step toward alleviating human suffering."[12]

I realized that the essential human quest expressed by our varied faiths is the same as that of the scientists I worked with over the years—to know ourselves. When it comes to studying the powers of the mind, most ancient religions and cultures, at their core, reveal a deep and holistic understanding of the mind. Yet sometimes their wisdom gets lost in rituals and rigid beliefs which, designed to provide a road map for a journey of inner exploration, can become the destination itself.

And this extends far beyond religion. Even in fields such as science, policy, and business, we often become so caught up in downstream details that we lose sight of our mission. As the Dalai Lama continued in his editorial, "Sometimes when scientists concentrate on their own narrow fields, their keen focus obscures the larger effect their work might have."[13] Thus, by looking at the same world through different lenses, we increase our potential to see new sights and discover new insights.

$$\sim$$

Luckily, the lens of neuroscience has made more progress in understanding the brain in the last few decades than in all the preceding years of scientific inquiry combined. Thus, even though our knowledge on the brain remains in its infancy, the little we have learned promises to transform the very foundations of how we view ourselves.

Ironically, while we are each in constant contact with our mind, it remains exceedingly challenging for scientists to access. Here, we will briefly explore a tool that provides preliminary clues on how our brain and body are linked (functional magnetic resonance imaging); and two emerging fields that are focused on studying how our mental activity can change our brain (neuroplasticity) and our body (epigenetics). Each of these areas, like any field of science, remains subject to significant debate among experts. Skeptics are rightfully concerned about the strength of correlations and the validity of the principles underlying them. Nonetheless, for minds seeking evidence, these fields provide the most scientifically grounded information available today and offer provocative insights on the power of the mind. For deeper study, vast explorations by experts in each field are easily accessible on the Internet and in other books.

Functional magnetic resonance imaging (fMRI) is non-invasive imaging technology used to study brain function. It allows us to visualize how blood flow through the brain changes in response to external stimuli and internal mental states. Using fMRI, researchers can correlate changes in activity across the brain with our understanding of their functions. For instance, in studies on meditation, fMRI shows that regular meditators can reduce activity in regions of the brain associated with stress and fear.

One of the most fascinating and provocative observations made with fMRI in recent years is that of *neuroplasticity*. In simplest terms, it implies that even an old dog can learn new tricks. Recent neuroplasticity studies reveal that neurons can generate new connections, or synapses, throughout life (*synaptic plasticity*). They also suggest that we can even generate new neurons throughout adulthood (*neurogenesis*). Activities such as physical exercise or learning new skills may promote neurogenesis, potentially even improving intelligence and slowing memory loss.

Studies on meditators show that, with increased practice, regions of the brain associated with compassion, empathy, and self-awareness can be strengthened; and regions of the brain linked to anger, stress, and fear impulses can be weakened. In essence, we are beginning to understand, at a scientific level, how our thinking patterns can change our brains.

Thus, when a negative thinking pattern holds us back, we can deliberately visualize and create a new, more positive path through our mind. Once we detour around an old way of thinking, shrubs grow over the old path. As we continue walking the new path, it becomes more prominent and easier to find and follow. In essence, this new science suggests that the mind is like a muscle and that training it can make it stronger and more resilient.

While fMRI and neuroplasticity shed light on our brain, the emerging field of *epigenetics* suggests our mental activity can also alter our genes, which encode the very recipes for creating us. Our genes are comprised of DNA, which is made up of four essential biochemical building blocks—known as A, T, G, and C—that combine in unique sequences. In our cells, genes are packaged into structures known as chromosomes. A complete set of 23 pairs of chromosomes defines our genome, which is our biological recipe book.

As any cook knows, much can happen between reading a cookbook and replicating the masterpieces depicted in its beautiful pictures. While nature is a master chef and its errors of significance are rare, we are learning that our "recipes" can be altered more than we previously realized. Recent provocative results from epigenetics studies imply that the expression of genes can change in response to environmental factors, diet, exercise, and even our state of mind.

Genes, like our neurons, likely have more "plasticity" than we previously realized. For instance, telomeres—the ends of chromosomes, which preserve the integrity of DNA as it replicates—shorten as we age, and their length is correlated with longevity. Shortened telomeres have been linked to increased risks for premature aging and chronic diseases, including heart disease, diabetes, osteoarthritis, and certain cancers. Recent studies suggest that this process can be accelerated or slowed by us: increased stress and negative thinking can shorten telomeres. Telomere shortening has also been correlated with childhood trauma, chronic inflammation, depression, and stressful experiences, such as caring for a chronically ill loved one.

Some early animal experiments suggest that such epigenetic changes may even be passed on to future generations. Reassuringly, researchers are also exploring how healthy eating, regular exercise, and improved mental health can prevent, halt, or even reverse these processes.

While our understanding of neuroplasticity and epigenetics is still nascent, these emerging fields suggest that our mental states may linger long after the fleeting passage of thoughts and literally shape our being. Neuroscience appears to be lending scientific credence to ancient wisdom that "we are what we think" and "we become our thoughts."

Experiments in Experience

Fascinated by these findings from medicine and neuroscience, I began to trace our knowledge on the mind back through time. On recent visits to India, in translations of texts dating back thousands of years, I discovered deep insights into how we can transform our mind, as I also did in explorations of healing traditions spanning the world's diverse cultures. So let us next tread into the vast field of practices designed to promote and restore well-being—referred to as alternative, complementary, or integrative healthcare. To simplify, I will refer to it as *wellcare* from here on.

While medicine tends to focus on pinpointed aspects of the body, wellcare takes a holistic approach, encompassing the entire system of body, mind, and being. One of wellcare's core tenets is: a healthy mind contributes to a healthy body, and a healthy body promotes a healthy mind. In contrast with the standardized world of healthcare, wellcare is a dispersed cottage industry of practitioners such as nutritionists, acupuncturists, and wellness coaches; yoga, meditation, qigong, tai chi, and Reiki teachers; and homeopathic or naturopathic doctors. Just as the complexities of science take time to understand, the lingo of meridians, *qi*, *prana*, and *chakras* can be equally perplexing at first encounter. For a mind seeking evidence, venturing into this field also requires cultivating patience, suspending skepticism, and maintaining a very open mind.

Predating the less-than-a-century-old clinical trials process, most of wellcare traces its origins to centuries of human trial and error. In the United States, wellcare resides mostly outside mainstream medicine, is sparsely covered by health insurance, and is mostly unregulated by the FDA. Yet 40 percent of Americans "use health care approaches developed outside of mainstream Western, or conventional, medicine for specific conditions or overall well-being," according to the NIH's National Center for Complementary and Alternative Medicine (NCCAM).[14] In addition, ancient healing practices such as Ayurveda in India and traditional medicine in China, South America, and other parts of the world continue to be the first line of care for many common, everyday ailments.

Most of us tend to arrive at wellcare at the suggestion of family or friends. Curiously, once I transitioned into researching and openly discussing my explorations in this field, my conversations in the same network of brilliant minds shifted. Longtime colleagues and friends—scientists, executives, doctors, entrepreneurs, and lawyers—started sharing tales of their own experiments and experiences in well-being and its gain and loss, as if whispering secrets that had become safe to share now that I was on the "other" side.

I had gleaned glimmers of this even during my investing days. An entrepreneur who was developing weight-loss surgery centers shared with me years ago his belief in the power of Reiki to heal and restore energy imbalance in the body. During the day, he expanded surgical centers as an executive. In the evenings, he altered patients' energy as a Reiki master. Another innovator, a doctor developing invasive technologies for treating obesity, had described how he had lost significant weight using a controversial diet. Both brilliant minds knew what they believed could not be validated by conventional clinical trials. Yet they practiced what they believed.

∾

Patients often arrive at wellcare because they find a holistic perspective lacking in today's superspecialized healthcare. Exasperated colleagues and friends have told me stories of becoming frustrated by prescription drugs and procedures that worsened their condition, or by doctors who reached the limits of their knowledge and had to say, "We don't know" or "This is the best we can do." On the other hand, compassionate doctors have also told me stories of patients who were dying of a curable disease but refused medical treatment because they were determined their alternative therapy would heal them. And it didn't.

The evidence-based approaches that guide medicine are so compelling because they help us reduce the world's complexity to testable hypotheses—such as whether one phenomenon creates another (causality) or whether they happen simultaneously by chance (correlation). Yet, because experiments need to be performed at a reductionist level of isolated, measurable variables, it is challenging for science to be holistic. Its greatest strength is also its greatest weakness.

For healthcare and wellcare to dismiss each other because one fails to make sense through the other's lens is limiting. Blindly following one approach when better alternatives exist is equally negligent. The idealistic mission of both fields is to enhance human well-being. So I wondered, *How can we best draw upon wellcare's vast repositories of knowledge on the mind?*

Wellcare lacks the validation of mainstream healthcare for several reasons. For one, it is difficult, if not impossible, to create placebos for many wellcare practices, since they involve complex "active" ingredients, multisensory experiences, or few easily measurable variables. We cannot measure our contentment level as we do our cortisol level. In addition, ancient origins and widespread use prevent most wellcare solutions from being patentable, leaving companies with few incentives to fund expensive validation trials. And, as I discovered, regardless of whether a wellcare solution is supported by data, if it is perceived to "work," most patients continue using it anyway. Firsthand experience becomes the most compelling data point.

While the placebo effect suggests that believing a "treatment" works makes it so, wellcare seems to systematically harness the power of this concept to heal the body through the mind. Wellcare emphasizes holistic well-being, and many of its practices incorporate sensory, experiential aspects that fully engross our mind. Yoga, meditation, massage, or acupuncture sessions often include relaxing music, calming aromatherapy scents, and warm, soothing lighting. Healers often use vivid language to evoke sensations of well-being. In essence, wellcare's practices encourage us to travel into our mind. With the power of direct experience, they bring volumes of theory to life.

I realized that the safest way to draw upon the wisdom of wellcare practices that strengthen the mind is to distill the essence of those practices that hold the potential of benefit and pose no risk of harm. This also begs the question, if a practice is harmless, what level of "evidence" of benefit do we need to use it with the same seriousness we afford cutting-edge innovations? I realized that if we believe a practice enhances our well-being, it does so by virtue of our expectation of benefit at worst and by means of its inherent effectiveness at best. It's a win-win. On top of this, if it is free and easy to use, we have nothing to lose by trying it out.

$\sim$

Eventually, the power of any idea rests in its potential for real-world impact—to create change. The placebo effect reveals the power the mind holds in creating positive change in the body. Neuroscience findings seem to validate that this process can change both our brain and our genes. Wellcare provides models for how we can harness the mind's power to initiate transformation. Yet I still wondered, how could we distill these disparate fields into a simple, unifying paradigm about the mind—a truly practical, easy-to-use tool to lead transformation not just in our health but also in our work, our lives, and in the world?

As I pondered the mind's capacity to both heal and hurt or lift and lower us, I realized that our ability to transform how we use our mind depends on understanding both what our mind is and what it can become. To visualize our full potential, as the wise physicist had suggested at the start of this chapter, we need a new lens through which to see our mind. And that's how the next chapter of this story emerged.

II. Map

CHAPTER THREE

Exploring the Mind

Every now and then a man's mind is stretched by a new idea
or sensation, and never shrinks back to its former dimensions.
—Oliver Wendell Holmes Sr.

The exploration we are about to begin is as old as humanity itself. From Plato and Socrates to the *Bhagavad Gita*, from the poems of Rumi, the words of Confucius, and the thoughts of St. Augustine to the writings of Henry David Thoreau, Mahatma Gandhi, and many others, we have been beckoned through the centuries to embark on life's simplest yet most powerful journey—the one that leads within—to pursue a singular mission: to know ourselves.

While we can fly around the world, and even to the moon, many of our long-ago ancestors were master explorers of the inner terrain. In fact, devoid of the myriad distractions of modern life, they might even have had an advantage.

You might be wondering, from a practical perspective, in our time-crunched, plugged-in 21st-century lives, what does it mean to "travel" within? Beyond grasping the science of how we are made or identifying our likes and dislikes, knowing ourselves is a journey of understanding how our mind operates through the diverse experiences of our lives. It is an ability to recognize why we are as we are and how we can become our best selves. It is not just contemplating and navel gazing; it is digging and creating the paths we wish to walk.

As I pondered the three defining experiences that catalyzed my journey into the mind—in the Finnish schoolyard, on the MIT street corner, and in the Sierra Nevada foothills—I started to discern a simple pattern. Thinking back to my days in Finland, I realized that our individual human journeys on earth begin by interacting with others to make sense of our physical world. We observe, experiment, learn; we acquire skills to meet our basic needs. The first phase of our journey is like a child's life.

The second stage of our journey consists of honing our intellect. We obtain an education and a career, we learn to become productive and acquire knowledge and wisdom from others. We develop ways to explain the world. The experience of standing on that MIT street corner, at the intersection of my education and my profession, embodied this phase for me. We can consider it an adult's life.

Yet, as I realized during that beautiful California dawn, there is a third journey we undertake in our lives. It is that of finding ourselves—our true selves. Through this journey we arrive at our own wisdom and learn to let it lead and define us. While we can get through our days without undertaking this journey, it is the one that breathes meaning into all our other travels—it elucidates life. I began to wonder whether this phase might best be equated with the metaphor of old age, which is when we often have a chance to gather and share wisdom. But then it suddenly dawned on me: These three journeys have nothing to do with age at all—they embody not the phases of our life but rather the states of our mind. We each have all three within us and we unlock our potential and unleash our power when we learn how to best use each state of mind to lead our life. This knowledge is akin to having a simple map to navigate our mind.

Maps have guided human quests, conquests, expeditions, and adventures since we began traversing the land and seas. Just as a map compresses mountains, oceans, and deserts into a few inches on a surface, this map for our mind distills its complexities to their most basic topography. Knowing how to use it gives us an enduring edge in all our travels. We gain new insights into how to use our mind, which begin to change the mind itself, thus catalyzing transformation.

So the idea we explore in this section is this: for most of our lives, when we are awake and alert, our mind exists in one of three states. I have named them as follows:

1.　The One-Dimensional (1D) Mind
2.　The Two-Dimensional (2D) Mind
3.　The Three-Dimensional (3D) Mind

How do we know in which state of mind we are at any moment? By recognizing its unique terrain. Once we learn the topography of each state, we can determine where we are and then travel to where we would like to be. The power of this idea rests in the principle that each state of mind is the optimal terrain for different decisions and actions in our lives. When we are in the right mental place for what we are trying to do, we attain our goals more easily, increase our chances of success, and reduce impediments holding us back. Rather than stumbling in darkness, we illuminate our paths. We improve our understanding of actions and decisions—those of others and our own. We learn to use our mind more effectively.

As our mind shifts, our life begins to do the same. By embarking on this journey, we gain firsthand experience in how change begins inside. So let's take a closer look at each of the three terrains.

The *1D mind* signifies our most primal animal mind and represents our impulses and instincts. It is committed to a singular mission—our survival—and thus strives to meet our basic physical needs: surviving in the face of threats, satiating hunger and thirst, avoiding pain, and seeking pleasure. Focused on the short-term, urgent, and immediate, the 1D mind is constantly on alert, ready to respond to threats at any time. It is guided by inputs from our senses and shaped by our experiences.

I have named this state the "one-dimensional" mind because it tends to move in one direction, with a singular intention. It leads us to run away from danger or toward pleasure. We can consider using the 1D mind as akin to driving a car through an old city—its potential paths remain confined to roads. Since we depend on the 1D mind for our survival and to meet our basic needs, we tend to default to it. This leads us to using the 1D mind much more than is necessary or even good for us. Overusing the 1D mind leads to mental stress, physical distress, and ultimately dis-ease. It can hamper effective decision making, sabotage success, and block transformation.

Most of us don't need to learn how to be in the 1D mind; we need to know how to get out of it. Once we learn to recognize its terrain, we can use simple yet powerful tricks to tame the 1D mind so it protects us when needed but doesn't control us when the 2D or 3D mind can serve us better.

$\sim$

The *2D mind* represents our rational, critical, and analytical thinking capabilities—our intellect. We rely on the 2D mind to guide our decisions and actions, and it is responsible for much productivity and progress in the world. The 2D mind helps build the structures and policies that govern our societies and lives. It is trained and honed by the systems designed to school us—formal education and professional training and development. The 2D mind is also the seat of our sense of identity or ego. Most of us define ourselves, and each other, through the lens of the 2D mind.

I have named this state the "two-dimensional" mind because it is like an explorer of a two-dimensional terrain. It surveys the landscape, absorbs information, and deliberates between alternatives. The 2D mind moves more slowly and systematically than the 1D mind and takes a longer-term view. We can compare using the 2D mind to walking through an old city. While a car remains confined to roads, by walking we can crisscross through narrow alleys, walk in and out of shops, and explore the city's nuances more deeply.

Honing the strengths of the 2D mind is not a subject we will cover here, since countless resources exist for that. We will explore how best to *use* the 2D mind and how to recognize its weaknesses, which can hold us back in subtle yet profound ways. We will consider how to avoid overusing the 2D mind, which can lead to analysis paralysis or limiting ways of looking at the world. When we optimize how we use the 2D mind, we can improve our decisions and avoid failures. We will learn when to rely on the 2D mind and when to let it go—to access the powers of the 3D mind.

The *3D mind* is the most mysterious state of our mind. It is the source of our insights and intuition, our creative and innovative potential, and our inner wisdom and truths. While the 1D mind is focused on protecting and feeding the needs of our body, and the 2D mind on honing our thinking faculties, the 3D mind leads us to realizing our highest potential. It is the foundation of lasting transformation. The 3D mind also promotes healing and compassion, and leads us to experiencing contentment and connection. Its truths expressed by one of us resonate with many of us.

I have named this state the "three-dimensional" mind because it can travel in three dimensions. If we return to our metaphor of exploring an old city, as opposed to driving or walking, the 3D mind takes us on a helicopter ride, revealing perspectives neither the 1D nor the 2D mind can provide. While the 1D mind focuses on the short term and the 2D mind on the long term, the 3D mind seems to transcend time itself.

Most of us don't learn about the 3D mind through formal education and training. Unlike the 1D and 2D minds, which we continuously use, our encounters with the 3D mind can feel random and unpredictable. Our intuition appears seemingly instantaneously, as flashes of wisdom or insight. Yet the 3D mind exists in a purely positive state within each of us. For most of us, the greatest challenge with the 3D mind is knowing how to proactively tap into it and trust its wisdom. We will learn how to access it anytime.

All three states of the mind are essential in our lives; yet each is best suited for different functions. When we need the 3D mind but operate out of the 1D mind, trouble emerges. Or when we can use the 2D mind but default to the 1D mind, we wonder why matters go awry. The map of this section is a simple diagnostic tool we can use to determine in which state of mind we are at any time. The compass of the next section guides us to tame our 1D mind, train our 2D mind, and learn to trust our 3D mind. Equipped with this map and compass, we can optimize and transform how we use our mind.

The power of this journey is that, whether we realize it or not, each step represents progress. As much as where we arrive, it is about what we absorb along the way. With each new exploration, we grow. Just as traveling the world enriches our perspectives on it, embarking into our mind deepens our understanding of our selves, each other, and our world. Each experience builds on prior ones, forming, reforming, and transforming us.

The beauty of this simple map is that implementing it in our lives does not depend on any regulatory approval, new infrastructure or technology, or additional money, resources, or time. It requires no policies or mandates to have an impact on the world. It just requires you, here, now—with an open mind ready for exploration and adventure.

Just as we don't need a map to walk the familiar streets of our hometown, once we learn the terrain of our mind, navigating through it becomes second nature. This knowledge stays with us for life and spells the difference between failure and success, between suffering and healing, and between trudging along in our health, work, and life and living at our highest potential. We come to realize that true intelligence rests not just in honing any one dimension of our mind but in balancing how we use all three.

Chapter Four

The One-Dimensional Mind

The only thing we have to fear is fear itself.
—Franklin D. Roosevelt

Imagine you are walking through a thick forest late on a summer night. The day's heat has settled into a balmy breeze, and the full moon shimmers through the canopies. Walking alone in silence, you hear mosquitos whirring, frogs croaking, and howling in the distance. As the moon casts a shaft of light on the path ahead, you glance at a snake slithering across. You stop, and—at that moment—you hear rustling behind you. Startled, you freeze, turn your head, and see a wolf staring at you. Before you have a chance to plot your next move, it starts charging at you, delighted that dinner has just arrived. Its glistening fangs glow in the moonlight, now it is less than a foot away, and...

Welcome to your 1D mind. The 1D mind represents our most primal impulses, including our survival instinct, and we depend on its swift reactions for self-preservation in the face of life-or-death situations. It is the most easily accessed dimension of our mind and it launches into action seemingly instantaneously. The 1D mind's virtues are clear—it protects us, and our life depends on it. Its vices often lurk like shadows in the recesses of our mind.

The chief problem with the 1D mind is that most of us tend to use it much more than is necessary, especially as true life-or-death predators have diminished in our safer 21st-century lives. Once our basic survival needs of food, water, shelter, and safety are met, the 1D mind is at a loss for what to do. It tends to treat all potentially threatening experiences with the same level of "seriousness," thus mistaking many situations we confront for matters of survival, when they are anything but that.

Bad traffic is not a wolf. Neither is a heated argument with a relative or colleague. Yet unless we teach it otherwise, the 1D mind leaps into action. Untamed, it takes charge when we face a difficult boss, the evening news, or a time-crunched day. The 1D mind is also in control when we avoid potentially unpleasant situations, resist change, or are angry, anxious, or afraid. When we know what is good for us but still don't do it, or know what is bad for us and still pursue it, we are likely driven by the 1D mind.

Yet we can't really fault the 1D mind. How could nature have known that we humans would change our ecosystems so much that the very feature of our mind designed to protect us would someday hold the potential for causing us the greatest harm?

Once we befriend our 1D mind, we can easily tame it so it protects us when our survival is at stake but does not rule over us when it can cause more harm than good. To begin, let us explore its main drivers: fear and hunger. Fear keeps us focused on avoiding threats and hunger on feeding our needs to ensure survival.

Fear

Fear can arise from a true external threat, from our perception of a neutral event as a threat, and even from imagining a threat. Just the thought of walking through a forest alone at night can arouse fear. Like other animals in nature, we are born with basic survival instincts, many of which need not be taught: most humans have an inborn fear of snakes. We also universally seek to avoid pain and suffering.

The 1D mind relies on inputs from our five senses to inform its activities. Upon suspecting danger, it rings our inner alarm bells, preparing us for two options: fight or flight—attack the predator or run away. Since both states require energy above our resting state, our body initiates biochemical and physiological cascades to prepare us for action.

Blood vessels constrict, restricting blood flow to the brain and gut and directing it to the limbs so the muscles are bolstered for action. Our levels of stress hormones such as cortisol rise, and insulin production increases as more glucose is guided into the bloodstream to serve as battle fuel. In medicine, these physical changes are known as the *stress response*. What they do to our brain, we can call the *distress response*. We actually become less intelligent in a 1D state, because the higher cognitive functions of the 2D and 3D minds are deprioritized. When the wolf is staring us in the face, we don't pause to ponder the origin of its species, examine its fangs, or try to determine when it last ate. We think less and act more.

In addition to being inborn, the 1D mind's reactions are also grounded in our own past experiences. This is biologically efficient. Once we learn a plant is poisonous or a situation dangerous, we remember and avoid it in the future. But this also leads the 1D mind to prefer being in the familiar and to resist change. *How*, it asks, *do I know the unknown potential is better than known certainty?* The status quo, whatever that might be, can feel safer and more comfortable than an unfamiliar future. The 1D mind does not encourage us to go out on a limb, to take a chance, or to pursue explorations that may "threaten" our survival. It can prod us to curl up like a hedgehog, roar like a lion, or eat more chocolate than we would ever need to live another day.

Fear sets the imagination on fire, skews our perspectives, and often creates unrealistic scenarios that have low or no probability of occurring. Phobias—overwhelming fears that tend to exceed the true danger presented by their cause—reside in the 1D mind. These can span specific sources (e.g., mice, spiders, and germs) and encompass experiences (e.g., being in crowded places, being alone, public speaking, and flying).

While fear is a forceful instigator for short-term action, when a threat is not real, the cost of capitulating to the 1D mind is high. Fear is a major contributor to frustration and failure in attempts at transformation. We are afraid of leaving one path to pursue another, or avoid facing change. Fear also plants seeds of questioning and doubt. We start to feel ambiguous about a decision or an outcome, which can erode courage and confidence. Fear often hijacks our mind by filling it with imaginary thoughts that hold us back. We can prove this to ourselves right here: Think of your three greatest, deepest, worst fears. Now consider whether each is grounded in factual truths about your current reality or in projected fiction about an imagined future. Most of us hold many fears that belong in the latter category.

Our fears can also be subtler. Sometimes our worst fears are not external ones but ones we avoid confronting within. One of the most pandemic fears holding many of us back from our highest potential is that of "not being good enough." Here "good" can embody wealth, beauty, power, intelligence, influence, or any other external metrics by which we can be assessed and sized up in a society. When we think we are "not enough," we are terrified of failing and worry about being called out in the world.

Such fears are ubiquitous and are even alive and kicking in many of the world's smartest and most successful people. The feeling of "not being good enough" may well be the greatest "disability" of our time, suppressing much human potential and leading many to walk paths that look externally successful but feel internally meaningless. We keep looking for ways to fill holes within, when the truth is that we are all whole.

Fear can become a barrier to progress even in the face of success. The more we have, the more we fear its loss. In large companies, organizations, and systems, cultures often become risk averse, encouraging preservation and stagnation, instead of disruption and transformation. When we feel we have little to lose, we often take greater risks. This is a powerful secret of success for entrepreneurs, inventors, and change leaders. Immigrants often leave everything behind to start a new life: with nothing to lose and not far to fall, they strive for the stars.

Fear also influences our decisions, from what products we buy to what jobs we seek, which relationships we enter and exit, and how we form and stand by our views and values in the world. We think a piece of art is rare, a job in short supply, or a person in high demand. We fear losing out and pursue and chase the objects of our desires. Bidding wars, auctions, and many competitions exploit the 1D mind. Yet we often neglect to stop and consider whether we truly need what we are chasing or if it is even good for us. This can lead us into lifestyle, career, and relationship choices that are incompatible with our inner truths or that take us further from our true meaning, purpose, and passion.

Fear often manifests through its close cousins—anger, anxiety, worry, and doubt. When we don't know how to process or express fear, these relatives often show up. Anger might be rooted in frustration with unfulfilled desires or unmet expectations. While anger tends to reflect fear rooted in our past or current circumstances, anxiety and worry are grounded in fear of the future.

Operating out of the 1D mind can become so second nature that we lose awareness of being in it. For instance, when we are in perpetual crisis-management mode—like entrepreneurs starting a company, professionals in stressful workplaces, and individuals overwhelmed by life's demands or personal traumas—we act primarily out of the 1D mind.

Yet we can either capitulate to fear or recognize it for what it is: a barrier to transformation and a limiting way of living in the world. Once we understand fear, we can release its grip over us.

Before we do so, let us explore the one other activity that engages the 1D mind: When it is not busy defending us, it occupies itself with feeding our hunger.

Hunger

The 1D mind strives to satisfy hunger to avoid starvation and ensure our physical survival. But just as with fear, the 1D mind can mislead us, because it is not good at knowing when to stop. Just as it exaggerates what it perceives as fear, the 1D mind's mission of overcoming hunger can easily extend to feeding our desires in countless forms.

When we derive pleasure from fulfilling such desires, they create positive emotions, such as satisfaction and joy. But when our impulses for pursuing wants are untamed, like a child in a candy store, the 1D mind easily overindulges. For instance, a voracious "appetite" can lead us toward chasing ever more of the same metrics that fear reminds us we don't have "enough" of, such as wealth, beauty, and power. Yet in the process we can lose sight of why we are "hungry" in the first place and how much we truly want.

For instance, greed, or uncontrolled hunger, can drive us to amass more than we would ever need. We forget what we are feeding within—and why. And this challenge extends beyond our lives. Companies focused on increasing revenues often aggressively market products that can do more harm than good or, in bids to continue increasing profits, compromise on best business practices.

At the individual level, sometimes our 1D mind seeks out pleasure to avoid or escape pain. Drinking alcohol to cope with stress. Eating ice cream to overcome a breakup.

Pursuing addictions in desperate attempts to get a break from our mind, to forget our thoughts, or to "lose" ourselves. Such short-term gratification can become addictive because the mind then requires increasing doses to experience the same relief. It becomes accustomed to craving short-term bursts of pleasure, instead of seeking long-term contentment. Furthermore, such temporary "solutions" often fail to address the deeper fears we avoid. They let problems fester.

The converse is also true. If something fails to give us sufficient pleasure or presents the potential for pain, we often avoid it. When individuals at the top of their game, whether they are star athletes, entrepreneurs, or leaders, are asked about the source of their success, most cite their capacity to pursue unpleasant tasks as a critical advantage. Many studies over the years also show that the childhood ability to control impulses, such as delaying gratification—effectively taming the 1D mind—correlates with greater adulthood professional and personal success.

Feeding the 1D mind's impulses may fill us in the short term but leaves us longing for nourishment in the long run. It explains why even those who amass vast amounts of fame, money, or power are still often left yearning for something more. Sometimes addictions even accompany such dissatisfaction. When we are driven by the 1D mind, we keep feeding its hunger yet feel neither full nor fulfilled.

Triggers to stimulate our hunger and feed our fears surround us. The advertising and marketing worlds have created an entire field called neuromarketing that caters to the 1D mind to try to influence our behavior. It feeds desires (e.g., beautiful models selling cars) and engenders a fear of missing out (often by feigning rarity).

The 24-hour news cycle also feeds off the 1D mind. Bad news is not just shocking; it's addictive. It puts our survival mode into overdrive. Once we are scared, the news can make us believe that by consuming more of it we can overcome the very fears it instilled in us in the first place.

Sometimes bosses resort to fear to get work done, leaders instill it to obtain support, and politicians rally it to gather votes. The most harmful consequence of excess fear and hunger is stress, which we explore next.

Stress

The storms on the seas exist for all of us. Why do some of us nearly drown or swallow too much water, while others swim safely to the shore? The ocean of life is filled with real and imaginary threats—fear of failure, doubt in our abilities, triggers for anger and anxiety, and countless other sharks. It is also filled with endless temptations. Why is it that some who "have it all" continue being stressed and craving more and others who have much less are happier and content?

Being stressed can, in simplest terms, be defined as being at the continuous beck and call of the 1D mind. The more we focus on what's in the water, the more it ensnares us. When we lose sight of the shore, we struggle with a sense of direction. And when we swallow too much water, we flail and drown more easily.

The way stress manifests varies among us. Some people eat more and gain weight, while others may acquire eating disorders and lose weight. Some develop elevated blood pressure, cholesterol, or blood sugar. Still others may suffer from an overactive immune system that causes allergies, asthma, or skin disorders. Some experience weakened immunity, which contributes to persistent coughs, infections, and likely even some cancers. Others take stress into their gut, where it becomes heartburn or bowel diseases. For others, it starts wreaking havoc in the mind and leads to phobias, anxiety, depression, and a host of other conditions.

We can also experience increased stress as a consequence of conditions the 1D mind views as threats, such as sleep deprivation, physical exhaustion without recovery, and life-altering crises, including deaths of loved ones or broken relationships. We have studied the negative effects of mental stress on our physical body for years. Chronic stress shortens telomeres, suppresses the immune system, leads to heart disease, reduces cognitive function, promotes insomnia, and increases mortality.

Stress is likely the most prevalent, expensive, and preventable "dis-ease" in the world. Of the 10 leading causes of death in the United States, stress likely contributes to eight (heart disease, cancer, chronic lower respiratory diseases, stroke, Alzheimer's disease, diabetes, kidney disease, and suicide).[15] Stress may also play a role in the last two. Our immune system is weakened under stress (contributing to the ninth cause: influenza and pneumonia), and we also become less alert and coordinated (instigating the tenth cause: accidents).

Stress knows no boundaries. Along with love, pain, joy, and sorrow, it is a universal part of being human. While poverty, violence, and unstable environments can be significant contributors to stress, anyone under the constant control of the 1D mind can experience stress and its associated diseases. In fact, the growth of stress seems to outpace many other metrics of modern human progress—despite ever-faster tools, many of us feel more time crunched and disconnected than ever.

A constant state of stress is no way to live. We had less choice millennia ago, when under the constant threat of predators, we depended on the 1D mind for survival. Today, we need not be at the mercy of stress in the face of 21st-century "threats" such as always-on gadgets and rat-race lifestyles. We forget how to take a pause, to look for deeper wisdom, and to recalibrate whether our life is serving us or we are slaves to it. Often, we sense something is off and think that there must be more to life than this. Contentment becomes tenuous and peace of mind elusive.

We often surrender to stress, accepting it as a part of life or thinking that we cannot do anything about it. While some causes of stress may be beyond our control, what we let them do to our body and mind is not. The starting point for such a shift is finding our faucets of stress so we can turn them off.

Finding Faucets

The most primal way in which the 1D mind speaks to us is by generating emotions within us. This encompasses our negative emotions, such as fear, anger, and anxiety. It also includes positive emotions associated with satiating hunger, fulfilling desires, and experiencing pleasure. Deeper positive feelings, such as contentment and serenity, are the domain of the 3D mind and we will explore them further when we travel its terrain.

The 1D mind stores our emotional experiences throughout life. Pleasant experiences create memories of positive feelings, and painful experiences hold triggers for negative emotions and stress. When stress manifests within us, it is often an outcome of our emotional history. At the mercy of triggers for the 1D mind, we react to circumstances rather than controlling how we would like to act. Sometimes these triggers can be traced as far back as childhood experiences.

Hence, understanding the 1D mind and finding our stress faucets rests in knowing why we do what we do and how our experiences and emotions shape us. Wellcare draws on this wisdom by incorporating explorations of root causes into many practices to heal patients. Practitioners often ask patients about personal, social, emotional, and other experiences that might be affecting their state of well-being.

Interestingly, healthcare has also studied this, through one of the most fascinating and powerful clinical trials ever conducted. Between 1995 and 1997, the US Centers for Disease Control and Prevention (CDC) and Kaiser Permanente collected data from 17,337 adults on their medical histories and childhoods, with the mission of understanding the impact adverse childhood experiences (ACEs) have on adulthood lives.[16]

The ACE study included a well-educated, middle class population drawn from Kaiser Permanente's San Diego members. The study was gender balanced and the mean participant age was 56. About 75 percent of participants had at least some college education and close to 40 percent were college graduates or higher. About 75 percent of participants were White and the balance included Hispanic/Latino, Asian/Pacific Islander, and African American participants.

While ACEs tend not to be discussed during a routine doctor's visit, and those who have them can experience deep stigma and shame in talking about them, ACEs are more prevalent than most people realize—much more. In the ACE study, close to two-thirds of adults (64 percent) had experienced at least one ACE, and close to 4 in 10 adults (38 percent) had faced two or more, with the overall study prevalence as follows:

1. Physical abuse: 28.3 percent
2. Household substance abuse: 26.9 percent
3. Parental separation or divorce: 23.3 percent
4. Sexual abuse: 20.7 percent
5. Household mental illness: 19.4 percent
6. Emotional neglect: 14.8 percent
7. Mother treated violently: 12.7 percent
8. Emotional abuse: 10.6 percent
9. Physical neglect: 9.9 percent
10. Incarcerated household member: 4.7 percent

Ironically, the sheer prevalence of ACEs should be reason enough for society to have open conversations about them and to obliterate their stigma.

The ACE study has continued to track the health of its participants and early data suggest that ACEs increase premature death and adulthood risks of developing many chronic conditions such as heart disease, chronic obstructive pulmonary disease, and depression. And they increase tendencies toward addictions and harmful behaviors. Even conditions such as anxiety or physical pain can often be traced to a past, unresolved stressful experience.

Based on their high prevalence, ACEs and their resultant lifelong effects may be the single greatest traceable and treatable root cause of stress and hence disease. When a part of us remains rooted in a past experience that caused pain or trauma, our entire being is unable to move full steam ahead into a different future. Such experiences engender fear and threaten us. The effect is resistance at a physical level as blood vessels constrict, leading to conditions such as increased blood pressure.

A more subtle effect takes place at the mental level: when we avoid confronting negative emotions or painful thoughts, we weaken our physical, mental, and emotional immune systems. Inner resistance can also manifest in response to adulthood traumas such as post-traumatic stress disorder (PTSD), unresolved grief, stressful relationships, and other such experiences. Trauma can make us feel disconnected not just from society but also from ourselves.

We sometimes avoid confronting past trauma or ignore it, hoping it will go away. It rarely does. Instead it comes back and taps us on the shoulder in quiet moments and can manifest in different forms: discontent, frustration, judgment, resentment, depression, anxiety, and addictions—not just to substances but also to work, different activities, and negative emotions. It can also lead to eating disorders, a fixation on physical appearance, and other ways of compensating for perceived inner defects by seeking outer, visible perfection.

Often the paths we follow in adulthood reflect desires to satisfy deep-seated needs that emerged from childhood experiences. Sometimes such paths are reactions to prior traumas leading to desires to obtain external validation, approval, affection, attention, and love. Some people, upon suffering a traumatic event over which they felt they had no control, become obsessed with controlling others. Others may develop obsessive-compulsive disorder (OCD), creating the illusion of controlling their environments. Or they become stubborn, closed-minded, or blindly rooted in their own beliefs, clinging on to an internally created reality that grants a false sense of security but keeps them from living their best possible life.

Some may unwittingly repeat cycles of addiction or abuse they witnessed in childhood. Others see themselves as victims, neglecting even those aspects of their lives over which they have full control and relinquishing their power to their circumstances, rather than their own actions.

While we cannot avoid pain and suffering in life, we can transform how they affect us, and as adults, we can turn off their faucets much more easily than we realize. The starting point for reducing the harmful effects of stress rests in understanding the origins of our distress. Even decades later, trauma can be resolved and healed once its root causes are diagnosed. A shift from identifying with the 1D mind to taming it leads to making peace with past experiences. We can disconnect from stress before it connects to us. Stress and its cascading effects on us become a choice similar to other daily decisions we make, such as what to eat, read, and watch on TV.

At this point, you may be feeling a bit uneasy or restless. Just reading about fear, hunger, stress, and trauma can start generating those feelings within us. But fear not—our next two sojourns are into the 2D and 3D minds, which guide us on paths from fear to courage, from hunger to contentment, from stress to peace, and from trauma to understanding. They lead us to recognize that the sheep we met at the start of this chapter was just wearing wolf's clothing.

Chapter Five

The Two-Dimensional Mind

We should take care not to make the intellect our god;
it has, of course, powerful muscles, but no personality.
—Albert Einstein

A few years ago, I was conducting research on a new startup developing a novel technology for treating wounds. Such research, which precedes each decision to invest in a company, is known as due diligence. It includes evaluating a potential innovation's merits—such as its scientific data, market size, and founding team—and weighing them against its failure risks.

One day, in the midst of due diligence on this company, I received a frantic call from the inventor of the technology. A few months earlier, he had partnered with an entrepreneur to raise venture capital and advance his technology. "He is undermining my technology," the inventor said of the entrepreneur. "He is questioning my data and doesn't appreciate the potential of my invention. Also, my intended ownership of the new company doesn't reflect the value my invention brings to it. I can't work with him. You'll understand, right?" We talked for a long time. The inventor had dedicated decades to this invention—it was the hallmark of his scientific career. Every argument he offered sounded reasonable, was backed by specific information, and warranted attention.

The next day, the entrepreneur called. "The inventor is not being reasonable," he said. "He is doubting my business strategy, is overestimating the market potential for his invention, and is not allocating enough company ownership shares to future employees. He thinks too highly of his technology. We can't work together. You'll understand, right?" The entrepreneur's detailed narration of the situation sounded equally logical and credible. He had started multiple companies and navigated the ups and downs of their product-development cycles. Recently, several startups had beckoned him to join them. They were both right, yet something had gone awry.

Over the years, I witnessed such conflict in countless variants. And it extends far beyond startups—managers, leaders, family members, communities, and nations, often limited to their ways of looking at the world, provide logical arguments to support the validity of their position and try to convince others and themselves of it. To help us "understand" what goes wrong in such situations, as the inventor and entrepreneur asked me, let's travel into the 2D mind.

Thought Factory

While the 1D mind works to protect us, the 2D mind makes us productive. It is the seat of our intellect and consists of our rational, logical, analytical, and critical thinking capacities. The 2D mind is the part of us that education—formal schooling, professional training, and lifelong learning—fosters and cultivates. Most of us, when not in the 1D mind, operate through the 2D mind.

The 2D mind's primary activity is to think—in fact, it loves, loves, loves to think. Although it can manufacture only one thought at a time, there appears to be no limit to the variety and volume of the 2D mind's output. Unlike the 1D mind, whose activities emerge as instantaneous or impulsive reactions, the 2D mind is slower and more methodical. It gathers information, analyzes thoughts, and strings them together to arrive at decisions and actions.

In fact, the 2D mind thrives on such deliberation. It loves to make pro and con lists and seeks to categorize and label the world into neatly organized systems. The 2D mind aspires to find rational and logical explanations for everything. It is not fond of randomness, mystery, ambiguity, and chance. Like a computer programmer, it seeks to reduce actions and activities into logic-based language and rules.

The investment world has extensively studied fear and greed, two of the most pervasive and dominant factors in investing decisions and the source of herd-mentality and panic-driven behavior, which we now know are instigated by the 1D mind. As a consequence, professional investors perform detailed due diligence with the 2D mind to guide decisions.

Due diligence is essentially a search for truths. Like good reporters and detectives, due diligence researchers seek to remove human biases to reveal a brutally honest look at raw, naked information. The process involves gathering vast troves of data, hunting for patterns within them, and mastering the art of asking questions. The more meticulous, rigorous, and thoughtful this process, the better the quality of the information obtained. Yet sometimes even the 2D mind's approach falls short.

While assessing a new innovation, I would usually interview experts and dig for truths in complex fields where multiple credible perspectives often prevail. Typically, I would find a top professor at a leading academic institution who would validate the importance of a new invention in treating a specific disease and offer supporting data. Upon further investigation, I would usually find other, equally credible experts who might refute that conclusion, often with their own evidence to bolster their position.

When faced with such dilemmas sometimes even the 2D mind fails to reveal clear answers. The 2D mind's strength is also its greatest weakness: it is limited to seeing the world through its logical, rational lens. To examine why, let's return to the analogy of traveling through an old city. While the 2D mind can explore it more intimately and methodically by walking through its alleys—as opposed to the 1D mind, which can only drive through its roads—even the 2D mind's capabilities are limited to two dimensions. It cannot obtain a bird's-eye view. Its thoughts, however highly developed, are confined to a street-level view of the city.

At this point, your 2D mind might be starting to question these words. The 2D mind does not like to confront its own limitations. If it senses the logic falling apart on a statement, it often begins to discredit the statement or shoot the messenger. But just ask it to be patient. We will soon understand why. Because the 2D mind thinks that it can rationally *think* its way through any challenge, it is unable to view the world beyond the parameters of its own thought factory. In the absence of logical labels and categories, or in the presence of seemingly irrational ambiguity, the 2D mind sometimes tries to rationalize and justify arguments, both to our advantage and to our detriment. While such an approach can help us make sense of the layers of an issue, it can also mislead us.

The 2D mind can lead us down a path of analysis paralysis, resulting in indecision or, even worse, the wrong decision. Also, when the 2D mind is fully occupied in churning out its own thoughts, it has no capacity to consider other possibilities. To understand why the 2D mind holds these two weaknesses—an inability to see beyond itself and a tendency to keep thinking—let's meet the boss of our thought factory: the almighty ego.

The Almighty Ego

The 2D mind is the seat of our sense of identity or unique self, commonly referred to as our ego. Our ego defines who we are, and most of us think (of course *think*, because that's what the 2D mind leads us to do) that we are who it defines us to be. The ego has a seemingly unending need to assert itself, and it loves to be in control.

While our ego defines the parameters of our outer identity—such as education, class, wealth, power, status, achievements, and our beliefs—it also exaggerates their importance. Viewing the world through its own lens, the almighty ego limits our ability to examine issues at an objective and holistic level. Thus by approaching any situation with our ego leading the way, we restrict our potential to experience and learn. It often fails to consider new and unfamiliar perspectives, which we might gather from others.

To establish a strong sense of self, the ego needs an "other" in whose context it can assert itself. Thus the ego exerts its influence through binary thinking, which is the 2D mind's tendency to create two sides to an issue. The intellect thrives on binary thinking because when presented with two sides, it has a chance to analyze to its heart's desire. Sometimes binary thinking can help us make sense of the world. It helps us teach children what is "good" and what is "bad." But more often than not, binary thinking over-simplifies the world and reduces our potential for deeper understanding.

When we look at the world as having two sides, the 2D mind drives us to identify with one and then to rationalize that the chosen one is the "right" one. Manifesting as "us versus them" thinking, this can introduce a sense of division and separation. This is what happened between the inventor and the entrepreneur we met at the start of this chapter. Each looked at the challenge he faced through the lens of his own experience, which established him in the right and the other side in the wrong. In binary thinking, each side may think that it knows better, that it operates on a higher plane, and that its partial view represents the full truth.

In extreme cases, the "other" side is rationalized as being unreasonable, irrational, or even less intelligent. Divisiveness can be further amplified by the ego's need to assert its righteousness, which often manifests as defensiveness, arrogance, and outsize self-importance. Each side may denounce the wrongness of the other, instead of questioning its own "righteousness." Such thinking helps the ego feel protected from being probed, threatened, or attacked. Yet when we let our ego drive our interactions with each other, we introduce a sense of separation that may start as subtle judgment, intolerance, or condescension but can easily become the cause of tension, conflict, and violence.

Such thinking can extend into societies and increase divisiveness between any two "sides" such as the rich and poor, the educated and illiterate, and the powerful and weak. It can also happen between liberals and conservatives, healthcare and wellcare, customers and companies, believers and nonbelievers, experts and everyone else. Yet in such "wars," often tragically perpetuated by a lack of deeper understanding and recognition of the other side, both sides are diminished. This can tear apart companies, relationships, families, communities, and even nations. Convinced they are right, both sides can be trapped, sometimes for lifetimes, in their ways of seeing the world. Often each progresses less on its own than they would by working together.

For instance, a sense of separation between the worlds of healthcare and wellcare holds us back from developing truly integrated ways of improving the lives of patients. Neither side can know the whole truth alone. Approaches that fix the human body and those that heal the human being are more powerful when combined than either is alone.

Imagine what could be possible if politicians in dueling parties recognized they were trapped by the weaknesses of their 1D and 2D minds and then prioritized working toward the progress of their nations over just focusing on their own parties' ideologies or interests. Or what we could attain if the world's religions agreed on a common goal: the uplifting of all humanity, regardless of the beliefs of individual humans. Or how communities could transform if conglomerates decided to pursue the right missions for the right reasons—promoting well-being and sustainability while building viable businesses—as opposed to bolstering profits at the cost of the greater good.

The more rooted in the 2D mind, or ego, we become, the more we seek to assert and preserve our known identity. The less sure it is of itself, the more prominently the ego seeks to be established. Defensiveness in the face of critique and taking issues personally instead of considering their context, are trademarks of the almighty ego.

The ego's insecurity can sometimes manifest as either arrogance or low self-esteem—two sides of the same coin. In low self-esteem, the ego obsesses about its unworthiness; in arrogance, about its worthiness. Yet arrogance can mask a deeper sense of unworthiness, often so subtle its bearer fails to recognize it. A grandiose sense of self holds back not just individuals but also organizations and nations.

Being rooted in the 2D mind becomes an obstacle to success in transformation, especially if our ego thinks its familiar sense of identity may be threatened. The more the ego fears its impermanence, the more it asserts its importance. The ego is terrified of failure. Traumas such as ACEs are often not openly discussed, because of shame, but shame is just fear held in the ego. It is fear of what others will think or say—what "labels" they will stick on us—and fear of confronting the ways in which we have labeled ourselves.

The 2D mind's thought churning is also tied to the ego. Eager to be heard and known, the ego continually pulls and tugs at us, telling us tales of its greatness and, at times, talking our ears off with random, useless thoughts. When it is not thinking, the 2D mind thinks that it ceases to exist, and that thought terrifies it. So it keeps thinking and thinking and thinking, often burning itself (and us) out to the point of utter exhaustion.

Without pauses for rest and recovery, our thought factory can go haywire. At times it might create a train of thoughts that look alike, or it gets stuck in churning out useless thoughts that we are then forced to mull over and over again. Sometimes it churns out thoughts faster than we can process them. These useless outputs become like "noise pollution" in our mind, drowning out our capacity for clear and productive thinking.

Imagine you slept for only an hour each night for days at a stretch, without giving your body a chance to rest. After a while, you would be exhausted. When we push our body too hard without giving it a chance to recover, it becomes weaker. In the same way, ceaseless thinking and perpetual stress reduce the endurance and performance of our mind.

At this point your 2D mind may be asking: If we tame and train the 1D and 2D minds, then who are we? If we are not thinking, then what are we doing? This is particularly puzzling to the 2D mind, which is what we are mainly using to read these words. If we are not defined by our ego, then how do we matter?

Beyond Binary Thinking

When I had just entered venture capital, a seasoned investor pulled me aside and said, "Now you will see how the sausage gets made." Once immersed in the art and science of conducting due diligence on potential investments, I came to appreciate what he meant. Understanding anything is a journey of becoming familiar with its messiness, in all its manifestations, and wading through it. Things are often not as they seem and when we label them as either perfect or defective, we usually don't know them well enough.

When we relinquish the thought patterns, language, and ideologies that keep us confined to our ways of thinking, we open ourselves to new possibilities. We surrender the belief that we know best. In human interactions, whether in making decisions, negotiating deals, or building relationships, to make real progress, we need to truly understand the other side. At times the truth may be black and white, but it is mostly somewhere in the middle. Our perceptions of it are, by definition, just partial perspectives. When we learn to listen to and honor an opposing view with the nurturing we give our own, we begin to understand the different shades of an issue and, in the process, often discover paths from one side to the other.

Let's return to the inventor and entrepreneur we met at the start of this chapter. Issues related to founding team dynamics are the "cause of death" for many potentially great startups and keep as many innovations from receiving investments as weaknesses in their inherent scientific or technical merits.

When two people or parties are engaged in a conflict, if it takes place at the level of the 1D mind, emotions and impulses dominate. Anger evokes reactionary thoughts and can lead to a full-blown fight—each side says and does things without thinking them through, which it will likely later regret. In the heat of the moment, we focus on words that "protect" us and help us fight off or avoid hurtful ones from others. We enter full-fledged survival mode. Sometimes we fear or avoid another human being when he or she seems to hold power over us, or more specifically, over our state of mind. The person becomes the object of our instinct for "fight or flight." The 2D mind can try to reason with the 1D mind, but when emotions run high, logic rarely prevails. When two people are engaged in a conflict at the level of the 2D mind, emotions may be cooler, and more rational discussions or arguments can take place. Yet in the 2D mind, the ego often dominates and leads us to rationalize that we are right.

The 2D mind can also foster passive aggression, which is grounded in the ego's fear. The ego attempts to protect itself by disengaging from conflict. Aggression is the "fight" response, and passive aggression is the "flight" response. While their manifestations are different, they are two sides of the same coin and neither leads to effective conflict management.

Most conflicts hold the potential for resolution, but to attain it both sides need to relinquish the grip of the 1D mind *and* the 2D mind. While both the inventor and the entrepreneur were "right" through the lenses of their respective 2D minds, they were "wrong" through a third lens—that of an objective observer who could bring perspective to the situation by understanding both sides. The 2D mind is great for gathering the information needed to coordinate a negotiation, but it is not always the best negotiator.

Training the 2D mind reduces the ego's hold over us and leads to true conflict resolution as we put ourselves in the other person's shoes, find common ground, and seek win-win outcomes. Sometimes by thinking less we attain more. When we look at our thoughts from a slightly amused distance, they cease to control us. We can view our life as a fascinating play in which we get to be the lead actor. We show up every day, play our part, and focus on doing our best without getting wrapped up in the outcomes that so thrill and rattle our ego.

This reduces binary thinking and a sense of separation. We become capable of greater compassion and kindness toward others and ourselves. We can embrace feedback, flaws, and failure. We find it easier to forgive others and ourselves and realize that the part of us that blundered or was bruised was just the ego. We realize that we are much more than the labels and categories of the 2D mind.

As we extend such positive feelings to others, we begin to focus on what is similar, not different. Understanding and empathy follow. Relationships are built this way, societies heal through it, and nations find peace in it. How do we get there? To find out, let's venture into the 3D mind. Are you ready for a helicopter ride?

Chapter Six

The Three-Dimensional Mind

You will ask me where I get my ideas. That I cannot tell you with certainty; they come unsummoned, directly, indirectly.
—Ludwig van Beethoven

The year I started business school, an unlikely new class, tucked away at Stanford's medical school, was created to probe a timeless question: Can innovation be taught? Its professors designed a yearlong program to study healthcare innovation and selected about two dozen students from the university's schools in medicine, engineering, design, and business.

Divided into small teams, the class was presented with a grand challenge in medicine: to invent solutions for the last unsolved frontiers in cardiovascular disease. My team included an aerospace engineer working on ingestible capsules for gut imaging, a product designer focused on novel home appliances, and a future surgeon. Besides the medical student, our expertise on the heart was limited to its poetic connotations.

Our team decided to focus on chronic total occlusions (CTOs)—the most challenging blockages in the heart's vessels, often not accessible to the minimally invasive guide wires, balloons, and stents used to open blocked arteries. Patients with debilitating CTOs often undergo open-heart bypass surgery, a much riskier and more expensive medical procedure.

Over the course of the year, leading product designers, inventors, entrepreneurs, and venture capitalists—a veritable who's who of Silicon Valley's brainpower—visited the class to share their wisdom and experience. They encouraged us to get in the trenches: to observe surgeons in action, to develop several crude prototypes, to rapidly test and iterate them, and to learn from each failure to make progress.

Our team organized creative brainstorming sessions that often transitioned to idealistic discussions on ethics, politics, and philosophy late into the night. We built simple devices and tried them out on chicken from the grocery store. We visited the medical school's cadaver lab. As I held a hardened artery—and felt it crunch between my fingers—the experience became worth a thousand textbook pictures, and the problem truly tangible. We tested our final prototype in a live pig in the basement of the Stanford hospital. After the class ended, we continued working on the project for another year, ultimately winning Stanford's university-wide business-plan competition.

What enabled a crew as motley as ours to innovate in a field of highly specialized experts? Years later I realized that re-inventing how we tackled the challenge transformed how we developed solutions. Our varied backgrounds led us to explore multiple problem-solving approaches and to generate a vast repertoire of potential solutions. By immersing ourselves in the trenches, we came to understand the nuances of the unmet medical need. Creative brainstorming techniques stimulated us to broaden our perspectives and maintain an optimistic, open mind.

For each of us, that class was among the best teamwork experiences of our lives, as we witnessed what our minds could attain together. Not only did the class confirm that innovation could be taught, but, as I realized years later, it taught us how: by leading us into the 3D mind.

～

The 3D mind is the most mysterious yet powerful dimension of our mind. It is the source of our creative and innovative potential and reveals our intuitions and deepest truths. We scarcely learn about it through formal education and tend to encounter it in spontaneous and sporadic ways. Even then, we rarely pause to understand it, and when we do, find that words remain limited in their descriptive ability.

Yet the 3D mind represents our capacity for finding inner wisdom, perspective, and a sense of purpose, passion, compassion, and contentment in life. If we consider the 1D mind as existing in the box and the 2D mind as thinking outside the box, the 3D mind removes the box. In the 1D mind we seek fish, and in the 2D mind the skill of fishing; in the 3D mind we explore nourishment beyond fish. The 1D mind resists transformation, the 2D mind understands it, but the 3D mind leads it. The 1D mind fears failure, the 2D mind analyzes and often learns from it, and the 3D mind embraces it as a necessary stepping-stone to future success.

From the point of view of the 3D mind, it makes sense that innovation can be taught. Consider that until science education became formalized in recent centuries, most scientists were creative household tinkerers who became masters at observing and thinking about the world. Over time, schools began to teach the scientific method. In recent years, the processes of innovation have begun to experience a similar revolution.

Yet even after taking that Stanford class, I was left with a nagging question. What *exactly* did we learn? I sensed that a thread from that class also wove through a sculpture class I took in college, through investment decisions I made over the years, and even through the yoga training program I more recently completed. Each experience, regardless of its subject matter, fostered an ecosystem that encouraged innovative, holistic thinking. Then it struck me. They all led to the same place—the 3D mind.

When we create ecosystems that foster the 3D mind, innovation emerges. This explains both why certain places become epicenters of innovation and why, regardless, we continue to witness remarkable feats of ingenuity in unlikely places around the world. Innovation ecosystems can emerge—and be created— anywhere. The 3D mind is present in each of us and any of us can tap into it—where we are, with what we have. By doing so, regardless of how we get there, we attain a seed for tapping into our creative potential and for unleashing transformation.

The journey into the 3D mind begins by understanding its terrain. As with learning to ride a bicycle, once we know how to access the 3D mind, we remember. And we can learn to ride this bicycle at any age.

3D, What Makes You 3D?

The trickiest trait of the 3D mind is that it is intuitively simple to understand when we are in it but impossible to fully grasp through the lens of the 1D or 2D mind. We cannot think our way to a 3D mind. Thus it can seem mysterious and difficult to access. Returning to our metaphor of exploring an old city, when we drive or walk through it, we can try to imagine what it must be like to fly over it in a helicopter. Yet if we have never flown, our language often remains limited to an on-the-ground perspective. Once we take such a flight and observe the vistas from above, many explanations become unnecessary. Once we experience our 3D mind we get to know it. Then, even when not in it we always remember that the 3D mind exists within us.

To try to grasp the 3D mind, it helps to move beyond the 1D and 2D minds. To prepare your mind for this journey, before we move ahead, take a deep breath, relax, close your eyes for a moment, and try to relinquish any mental activities that the 1D or 2D mind might introduce to distract you: judgment, fear, questioning, overanalysis, or distracting thoughts. For the next few pages, just follow along and try to stay in the moment word by word.

It helps to remember that being in the 3D mind is the most fundamental essence of being human: a state of contentment and meaning, and one we spend many other journeys of our lives chasing. In the 3D mind we experience profound serenity. The fears and hungers of the 1D mind subside, and the thinking machinery of the 2D mind slows down and sometimes even pauses. We lose track of the passage of time and become immersed in the present. We might first experience this state as fleeting flashes of absolute immersion in a moment. With practice, and over time, we can access it more deliberately.

The 3D mind alters the state of our body and our being. It is a powerful antidote to stress and counters the harmful side effects of the 1D mind. The stress response subsides, our breathing becomes deep and relaxed, and the muscles of our body unwind and release tension. Stress-related hormone levels are lowered, and the cascades that take us into survival mode—elevated blood pressure, increased blood sugar, and reduced blood flow to the brain and gut—begin to be reversed. In the 3D mind we are freed of inner resistance. Restlessness recedes and relaxation enters. Through its positive and powerful effects on the body, the 3D mind promotes healing and feelings of well-being. Being in the 3D mind can help reduce the severity of many chronic diseases and even overcome 1D mind–related conditions such as addictions and insomnia. In the 3D mind we feel safe, peaceful, and fulfilled within.

The 3D mind also counteracts the weaknesses of the 2D mind. By slowing down (and sometimes halting) our thought factory, the 3D mind allows us to surmount analysis paralysis, attain deep perspective, and uncover new solutions. In the conflict between the inventor and the entrepreneur in the prior chapter, using the 3D mind helps us recognize that the initial reactions on both sides—fear, judgment, and the desire for "flight"—were consequences of the 1D and 2D minds.

When two people engage at the level of the 3D mind, each seeks common ground and ways to harmonize their thoughts, words, and actions. They become two souls engaged in the same currents of life. The focus shifts to the greater good, the higher vision. Then the conflict is less about the fight—venting anger or protecting one's ego—and more about resolution. Compassion, empathy, and understanding enter the conversation and allow each side the opportunity to understand and be understood by the other side. This simple yet seemingly rare act in human interaction is the starting point for virtually all peaceful conflict resolution. With the wisdom and perspective of the 3D mind, founders in conflict can focus on their shared mission, the value each brings to the company, and their potential for transforming healthcare by working together.

In essence, the 3D mind leads us to zoom in and out of situations to attain greater insight or perspective, thus shifting how we approach challenges. In this way, we discover root causes and can then turn off faucets or plant seeds for lasting transformation. Change rooted in the 3D mind, faces less resistance. It emerges from within.

When we are trapped in a dilemma or a difficult decision, we often analyze and agonize. Answers we arrive at through the 1D and 2D minds may bring uneasiness, resistance, doubt, or fear. Using the 3D mind, we can shift our approach. Sometimes, to answer our deepest questions, it helps to gather the relevant information and then mentally "walk away" from the dilemma itself—to release it from our thoughts. Then the 3D mind has a chance to reveal our wisdom to us.

When we access the 3D mind, often it is as if an epiphany strikes, clarity emerges, and doubt evaporates. In fact, many of our best and most meaningful ideas, intuitions, and insights seem to just appear—their origins an elusive mystery. We say, "It came to me in the shower, while going on a walk, or as I was waking up." Often such moments are preceded by a brief pause. We say, "And then a lightbulb went off," or "Suddenly a flash of insight appeared."

Albert Einstein often spoke about this process explaining how, "a new idea comes suddenly and in a rather intuitive way."[17] Once while discussing creativity with a poet, he said, "The mechanics of discovery are neither logical nor intellectual. It is a sudden illumination, almost a rapture."[18]

How can an idea just appear? It doesn't make sense to the 2D mind. It can't, because the 2D mind is confined to its ways of thinking. While a new idea seems to come out of nowhere, it does come from somewhere—it emerges from the 3D mind. What happens is that we reach a moment of stillness when the 2D mind becomes quiet, allowing the 3D mind's creativity and wisdom to emerge.

Many inventors, artists, and writers describe the creative process as a mysterious journey, even beyond their own full comprehension. Creativity often seeks a source for inspiration, which is what the Greeks referred to as a muse. Many artists speak of special rituals, inspiring places, and uplifting people who awaken something within them. Ludwig van Beethoven continued the words that began this chapter as such, "You will ask me where I get my ideas. That I can not tell you with certainty; they come unsummoned, directly, indirectly,—I could seize them with my hands,—out in the open air; in the woods; while walking; in the silence of the nights; early in the morning; incited by moods, which are translated by the poet into words, by me into tones that sound, and roar and storm about me until I have set them down in notes."[19]

We may seek different muses in the world, but they have the same ultimate effect of taking us into the 3D mind. Then we experience the same world with sharpened and heightened senses—the same sights reveal new insights, and old experiences become fresh explorations. We realize that we have fewer limitations than we think and that those we imagine, by definition, exist only in the mind. We find a new world, because we discover our world anew.

The 3D mind is often the answer when other explanations fall short—such as a patient experiencing miraculous healing, a scientist making a trailblazing discovery, a poet weaving words that echo the depths of humanity, or an artist creating work that strikes a chord across nations. The ideas and insights that emerge from the 3D mind tend to feel right in the depths of our being and we don't second-guess them. In this way the 3D mind leads us to finding our passion, inspiration, and purpose—to discovering meaning in life.

3D, How Do You Work?

Sometimes life's circumstances force us into the 1D mind. When our life is severely threatened—in the face of danger or in a state of pain or physical suffering—the body's survival needs are urgent and critical. Yet beyond such circumstances, we tend to spend more time in the 1D and 2D minds than necessary, often causing ourselves needless mental suffering. Entering the 3D mind is a journey of letting go of the weaknesses and limitations of the 1D and 2D minds. When we are not led by fear and hunger, and as we loosen the grip of our thoughts and ego (i.e., who we think we are), we connect to our simplest and deepest essence (who we truly are) and discover who we have the potential to become. When the 1D or 2D mind takes center stage, the 3D mind goes backstage. Once those two clear the stage—when we are at peace and cease thinking—the 3D mind tiptoes onto it.

Mahatma Gandhi once told a story that described this: "I visited a Trappist monastery in South Africa. A beautiful place it was. Most of the inmates of that place were under a vow of silence. I enquired of the Father the motive of it and he said the motive was apparent. 'We are frail human beings. We do not know very often what we say. If we want to listen to the still small voice that is always speaking within us, it will not be heard if we continually speak.'"[20]

To hear our intuition's gentle whispers, we have to ensure that the instinct's roars and the intellect's loud chatter don't overpower it. As we learn to tame the 1D mind and train the 2D mind, the 3D mind begins to reveal its powers. This is disconcerting to striving, hardworking minds and is one of the most counterintuitive insights about ourselves. We can realize some of our greatest powers by doing and thinking nothing. The less we let our impulses drive us, and the less we think and analyze, the more easily we access the 3D mind. Less becomes more. This explains why solitude can be so powerful for creative work. Thoreau wrote of its virtues while in nature by Walden Pond. Einstein described solitude as the source of his most creative moments. Nelson Mandela was thrust into it during years of imprisonment.

Also, when athletes speak of being "in the zone" or artists experience a state of "flow," they are in the 3D mind. When immersed in an activity, whether it is participating in a sport, creating art, playing music, or composing poetry, we lose track of time and place and forget ourselves. During such moments, we feel that anything is possible. We enter a different state of being, experience a shift in our mind, and access our peak potential.

In the 1D mind we are followers, in the 2D mind we can be leaders, but in the 3D mind we become transformers. When the 1D and 2D minds lead our lives, the focus is on tangible aspects, measurable achievements, and material possessions. Even when helping others, we give of our finite, forever limited assets—money or time. When the 3D mind leads, we focus as much on inner assets—kindness, compassion, comfort, love, and the power to help others.

When we give these "assets," we often rediscover their vast reservoirs within ourselves. This explains why many say that engaging in charity is often a selfish act—we gain more than we give. Each time we give from within, we become richer. When giving from the 3D mind, we light a spark in others that, like a candle, can give light to countless others. This spark is the essence of being human. No money or power in the world can buy it. No red carpet leads to it. We each have it already. Sometimes we just need to rediscover it within.

3D, Where Does Your Power Come From?

While the 1D mind focuses on our physical needs, and the 2D mind concerns itself with mental matters, the 3D mind represents a connection to the firepower that has fueled and lifted humanity through the ages—our inner energy. Like other forms of energy, our inner energy is intangible yet real, which makes it tricky to explain. Despite increasing advances, science remains limited in its ability to study it and we cannot put it in a test tube or measure it. In fact, not much about living in the 21st century gives us an edge over our earliest ancestors in studying it. Like the force of gravity, we cannot touch, see, hear, smell, or taste this energy. We experience it when we are in the 3D mind. Once we feel it in our being, we need little further explanation.

We need only to have felt deep love; been moved by inspiring words, beautiful music, or a sunrise; or lifted by true joy and passion to know that it exists. When we say we know something in our hearts, sense it in the depths of our being, or feel it in our bones, we speak of this energy. When we recognize others' words as our truths, feel fulfilled, or perceive that we are living our mission, we are tapping into our inner energy. In our encounters with it, we often feel transformed. It drives us, fuels us, and connects us—to our selves and to each other.

Our inner energy has borne many names through the ages. Wellcare refers to this energy by as many terms as there are practices—it is our inner being, vital essence, life force, true nature, *qi, prana*, to name just a few. It is the energy that wellcare practices seek to harness to heal us from within. Meditation and mindfulness help us directly access it. Yoga, which means "union" in Sanskrit, aspires to unite us with it. Reiki and acupuncture are designed to rebalance this energy within us.

At a more fundamental level, our inner energy is the expression of our truest essence. Love—in the most universal sense—is one of its most powerful manifestations, but it is even more vast than that. This energy weaves through human attempts at understanding ourselves from our earliest beginnings. Religions refer to it when they speak of our soul, spirit, or the presence of spiritual energy or god within. Spiritual leaders and healers have spent millennia trying to describe it. Their very mission, one might argue, is to help us access it.

Poets, musicians, artists, and writers have invested lifetimes in trying to express it. Ever beyond our full grasp, its precious glimmers appear in their poems, songs, paintings, architecture, and performances. This is why art and music hold the capacity to stir us so deeply, to strum the strings of our being, and to bring out the songs within us. They speak to us at a level beyond our thinking mind. Often we cannot describe how and why, but we feel it. The 3D mind resonates so powerfully between and among us because it reveals humanity's deepest truths.

Sometimes even when we read translations of ancient texts, such as *The Yoga Sutras of Patanjali*, or the words of philosophers from centuries ago, we feel as if they echo the truths of our hearts. We sense they understand us. This is because they understood themselves. When we grasp our own essence, we unlock the essence of humanity.

As we connect with others beyond the superficial differences that divide us, we realize a deep sense of unity and universality. We recognize that each one of our journeys is part of all others and is woven into the grander journey of humanity through the centuries. We see any true mission and purpose we pursue as a shared mission of humankind: not just to lift ourselves but to raise all of us.

When our work does not meet such a purpose, we often feel disconnected. And when it does, even the smallest effort on our part ripples into the world. If we each spent more of our lives in the 3D mind, imagine where the world could be. Once we know the 3D mind within us, we recognize it in others as well.

This principle embodies the living guide of most great souls who walked the earth. Spiritual leaders such as Jesus and Buddha lived by and taught it. When we serve others with empathy, compassion, and love, especially those who need our help the most—children; elderly people; the sick, neglected, and dying—we sense the truths of the 3D mind. We begin to see all as fundamentally the same. We see others as holding the same seeds of goodness within and as being part of us. We recognize that the inner energy is the same in all of us.

In a noise-filled world, connecting to our inner energy appears to be an increasingly rare experience. Yet we depend on it to truly *live* our lives. The 3D mind brings a sense of mission and meaning to life. Once we learn to trust its powers and access its wisdom, we discover new paths to our highest potential. That is because the 3D mind leads us, in the most fundamental way, to knowing our true selves.

3D, Are You Perfect?

Of course the 1D and 2D minds need to ask this question. At this point they might be feeling a bit intimidated or confused by the powers of the 3D mind. The 3D mind knows that nothing is perfect and that everything just is. Yet while this concept is intuitive for the 3D mind, it warrants explanation to placate the 1D and 2D minds. The 3D mind is not a panacea to all our life's problems. But, when we tame our 1D mind, train our 2D mind, *and* learn to trust the powers of the 3D mind, we attain an enduring edge in how we use our mind. A well-balanced mind leads us to unleash our full potential. For that, all three states of mind are necessary and most of us access and trust our 3D mind much less than serves our lives.

At the same time, it helps to remember that the 3D mind cannot take on the vital protection role that the 1D mind plays. It can, however, help to tame the 1D mind so that it springs into action only when needed and learns to sit still when it would just cause mischief. The 3D mind also respects the talents of the 2D mind. In fact, it depends on the 2D mind to enrich its powers. Returning to the metaphor of exploring an old city, the 3D mind flies above it, gathering patterns and insights. Yet those are most meaningful when they complement the 2D mind's detailed on-the-ground inputs. Else, even the 3D mind might draw conclusions based on limited knowledge. This is a crucial point.

While the 3D mind has no inherent weaknesses, its wisdom, intuition, and insights are best harnessed alongside the strengths of the 2D mind. Intuition absent information can lead to blind faith and a false sense of confidence in our intuitive abilities. An overreliance on hunches about situations or future actions can lead us to avoid confronting hard truths or to delay developing concrete action plans grounded in accountability. While the 3D mind reveals our wisdom to us, it needs the strengths of the 2D mind to convert our insights into new realities. Then we can access our true intelligence, attain breakthroughs, and discover paths to transformation.

To harness the power of our mind, we need to know how to both recognize and navigate through all three terrains. During this journey into the mind, I came to realize that the healthcare innovation class I took in business school did this remarkably well. As students, we observed the world with an open mind, gathered data to inform our process, and then tapped into our innovative potential. In fact, the more I have studied the processes of innovation, the more convinced I have become of the powerful role of the 3D mind in creating and leading it in our world.

3D, How Do You Innovate?

Today, many companies, cities, institutions, and governments are trying to establish methods, metrics, incubators, and ecosystems to foster innovation. We see innovation as a beacon of hope for solving our greatest challenges, such as creating jobs, educating children, and promoting healthier societies. The origins of innovation often seem mysterious but creativity is not a secret for a few of us. Its seeds are within each of us. It thrives in particular ecosystems, external and internal ones.

Before we invest significant resources in building systems for generating innovation, it helps to step back and consider which dimensions of our minds such systems will foster. Since it seeks safety and survival, the 1D mind is not designed to be creative. Fear and hunger are poor motivators for spurring innovation. Carrots and sticks may offer incentives but rarely catalyze breakthroughs. The 2D mind provides the necessary knowledge to innovate but still tends to operate in rational, predictable ways. Thus, rigid metrics, restrictions, and rules around innovation often stifle the very processes they are designed to foster. The mind is most creative when it is free to deviate, roam, and explore in the

3D state. This explains why the most creative work often takes place at the fringes, edges, and intersections of worlds, and why the greatest change agents often come from the outside to transform an industry, a culture, or a society.

Mahatma Gandhi did not begin his career as a politician. Yet his experiences of racism while practicing as a lawyer in South Africa inspired his quest to free India from British rule. Albert Einstein, rejected from several academic positions, became a patent clerk. Yet his spare-time passion for physics led him to revolutionize the field and become one of its most brilliant minds. These are just a few examples. Such disruptors are everywhere, because a 3D mind can lead transformation anywhere.

Small companies often out-innovate larger ones because they are nimble and create ecosystems that encourage creativity and eschew inhibitions of expertise. For startups, the cost of failure is low, and in a world that often fears failure, this becomes a competitive advantage. Time and again, we find that simple ideas conceived outside complex, bureaucratic systems provide transformational solutions.

Expertise can become a hindrance in accessing the 3D mind, because the 2D mind's ego and information advantage become dominant. And entrenchment can breed complacency. Large organizations often become trapped in rigid thinking and value conformity more than breakthroughs. Established brands, reputations, and cultures fear disruption. This also explains why throwing more money at challenges often fails to create more innovation. In fact, often it has the opposite effect by restricting resourcefulness and outside-the-box thinking. As we consider how to lead, innovate, and invest in solving the world's greatest challenges, beyond focusing on resources and policies, we need to direct our attention to the root cause or faucet of innovation—how we use our mind.

The most significant stimulus the world needs today is a mental one. Once we learn to navigate our mind, we can transform how we use it. We can live the same life at a higher level. The more we access this wisdom, the greater our capacity to change our lives and the world. We now have a map for this journey. All we need is a compass to guide our new adventures.

III. Compass

Chapter Seven

Navigating the Mind

Be a Columbus to whole new continents and worlds within
you, opening new channels, not of trade, but of thought.
—Henry David Thoreau

O n a cold winter morning in early December 2012, I
was rushing to a policy discussion on mental health
on Capitol Hill. Amid increased awareness of the toll of
mental disorders, I expected the room to be packed and
wanted to get there early. When I walked into the cavernous
marble-pillared hall in one of the Senate office buildings, a
few dozen people were scattered across it, scarcely filling
a quarter of the seats. Those absent that day missed an
extraordinary story of personal transformation.

After an opening presentation on the adverse childhood experiences (ACE) study covered in Chapter 4, a
young woman took to the podium to tell her life story. She
described how she had first experienced trauma as a little
girl and had, by young adulthood, suffered from virtually all
of the traumas identified in the ACE study: abandonment,

violence, addictions, and repeated neglect and abuse. It was heart-wrenching—one sliver of her experiences could tear a life apart, and she bore a lifetime of them. She spent her early adulthood shuffling in and out of prisons and mental-health and social-support systems and described how she was relentlessly asked, "What did you do?" She felt neglected, abused, and discarded—as if she didn't matter.

Yet one day, when she had just reentered the system, a support worker asked, "What happened to you?" That single, simple question, she said, became the starting point for turning her life around. Why? Because, as she told the goose bump–riddled audience, instead of blaming her for her life, the question helped her view her experiences as events that happened to her but did not define her. As long as she identified with her suffering, she remained in the 1D mind's survival mode, thinking that her past experiences defined her future options. She focused on just living another day. The question posed to her made her aware that there was another way to view her life. Then, with the help of support networks, she could tap into her 2D and 3D minds, gain perspective and a longer-term view, and imagine other possible futures. She found hope.

This story also reveals powerful insights when considered from the perspective of the systems and caregivers designed to help this young woman and others trapped in circumstances like hers. When policies and systems view her through the lens of the 1D mind, the focus is on ensuring she does not endanger survival—that of others and her own—and the solutions are often short-term and surface-level, such as jail. Through the lens of the 2D mind, we often design policies—carrots and sticks—such as social service programs to address the harmful consequences of risky behavior. We also tend to attach labels to a person and say, "She's an addict" or "He's violent." Yet the humans governing and operating our systems hold immense power to help catalyze transformation in others. As a society, we can harness this potential to create more opportunities that can turn lives and communities around.

Through the lens of the 3D mind, we see another person not as a damaged body or mind but as an eternally whole human being. Instead of saying she *is* a problem or that she *has* a problem (as the 1D and 2D minds would), the 3D mind says she *experienced* a problem. Here the word "problem" can stand for any other circumstances or experiences that can cause suffering, such as addictions, trauma, and other mind-related anguish. The 3D mind looks beyond the labels of the problem and asks, *How can we work together to help you navigate your way out?* In the 3D mind, when we face each other we realize, *You are human, just like me. In life's birth lottery, I could have been in your place or you could have been in mine. You have a heart and soul, just as I do. You have feelings, seek dignity, and strive for the same ultimate safety, peace, contentment, love, and meaning in life as I do. We each want to matter. Why did your life take such turns? In the grand web of humanity, your problems are as much mine and my privileges as much yours. How can I help you heal? How can we restore your dignity together?*

Recognizing that a trauma controls the 1D mind helps us confront it with the objectivity of the 2D mind and the wisdom of the 3D mind. At another conference on the mind I attended earlier that year, a panel of military veterans described how trauma and PTSD can be challenging to overcome because their stigmas hinder acceptance and, hence, healing. One panelist suggested how reframing a problem can help. She said, "We are ordinary people who have been through extraordinary events, and we are reacting accordingly—that's it."[21]

The simple shift from treating someone as a problem moving through a system to seeing him or her as a human being the same as any other becomes the starting point for the journey of healing and transformation.

$$\sim$$

All three states of mind are vital in our mental toolbox as we travel through life. Yet we each tend to lean on some states of mind more than on others. Some people are more impulsive, others more analytical, and still others more intuitive. Knowing when to use which dimension of the mind helps us pull out the hammer only when it is truly needed and not when the screwdriver could do a better job and the hammer might just inflict harm.

Navigating our mind in this way begins with recognizing where we are, deciding where we want to go, and then finding our way there. If you were dropped a few miles from the edge of a forest on a cloudy day, how would you know in which direction to move to get out of it? Just having a map is not enough. We need a tool to orient us and to guide the way. This section offers us a compass for our mind to navigate through its terrains. Since most of us tend to default to the 1D or 2D mind, this compass shows us how to get out of each. And because the 3D mind appears most challenging to access, it shows us the way there. Once we learn to use this compass, we can travel our inner terrain with the ease of an experienced explorer who sees even the world's most treacherous terrains as holding the potential for adventure. Here are the key elements of this compass:

1. The way to taming the 1D mind is with *awareness*. Awareness introduces mental space that gives us an opportunity to recognize that we don't have to live out all our fear, hunger, and trauma. It reminds us that we are not solely defined by our circumstances, our states of mind, or our feelings, and that we can control and change each of them. We attain such awareness by *being positive*. Positive thoughts lift us out of fear and take us beyond survival-driven thinking to suggest other possibilities. As we increase our awareness and bring more positivity to the 1D mind, we tame it.

2. The path to training the 2D mind is *perspective*. Perspective leads us to consider both sides of a conflict, helps us to remember that we are more than our ego-defined identity, and reminds us that there is more to life than we "think." We obtain perspective through *focus*. Focus concentrates the powers of our mind on what matters. When we attain focus, we learn to operate beyond the 2D mind's binary thinking, to pause our thought churning mental factory, and to reduce the dominance of the ego.

3. The journey into the 3D mind begins by learning to recognize and trust it. This is the greatest challenge with tapping into the 3D mind because it functions in

subtle and quiet ways. As we tame the 1D mind and train the 2D mind, we clear the path to the 3D mind. At the same time, we can access it more proactively with *positive focused energy.* Just as magnetic energy guides a compass needle to point north, positive focused energy is the energy field that guides us toward the 3D mind. Why? Positive thoughts take us out of the 1D mind, and focus allows us to escape the 2D mind. When our inner energy is positive and focused on what matters, it gains momentum, strengthening our mental power. This leads us into the 3D mind. Positive focused energy is a simple, powerful way to access our mind's full potential.

Before we journey on, let's stop for a moment to consider the power of having such a compass. Our lives are filled with contradictions. Sometimes the 1D mind drives us to pursue an impulse that the 2D mind knows is not good for us. Or the 2D mind carries us to a logical decision that doesn't feel right to the 3D mind. Often we are told to "trust our gut" or "trust our instincts." Yet what do we mean by "gut"?

How do we know whether something "felt in the gut" is emerging from instinct or intuition? Both our instinct and our intuition appear spontaneously, unlike the slower analytical thinking that emerges from the 2D mind. Thus we can easily confuse the instantaneous gut feelings of our instinct with those of our intuition. If a thought appears in a state of high emotion or impulse, such as hunger or a desire; or if it holds fear, anxiety, or restlessness; or if we want to pursue it without thinking about the future, it is likely driven by instinct. If a thought emerges in a state of serenity, reflects our inner wisdom, and embodies what we know is good for us, it emerges from the intuition. Yet our intuition can best guide us after we have used the 2D mind to gather sufficient knowledge about a decision's pros and cons. If we don't use the 2D mind, or if we think we can just rely on our "gut," our inner wisdom operates on limited knowledge.

Becoming aware of this nuance regarding our different "gut" feelings holds as true for what we seek as for what we avoid. Often inner uneasiness is driven by the 1D mind's fears, which have been generated by past experiences and have nothing to do with what is before us. We have a bad experience with a person wearing a red hat and decide to avoid all people who wear red hats. While such shortcut thinking might be efficient for the 1D mind, it can lead to judgment and prejudice. We may brand others with the labels of our own ignorance and write off vastly diverse communities, religions, or cultures based on our limited experience. Yet in the process, we deprive ourselves.

Thus before we get up and fight our battles in the world, it helps to consider what is going on in our own minds. For instance, our fear might be driven by a childhood event that bears no resemblance to our current reality. We can step back and consider the root causes of our reactions: *Why do I feel this way? Am I confronting reality or engaging in conjecture?*

One way to explore this nuance is to consider that we can pick up the same book at different times and have utterly disparate experiences with it. The words don't change. It is our mind, and its state of being, that determines how we react and what we connect with or disregard. As you read about the three states of mind in the prior section, some might have resonated with you more than others. The same happens with experiences we encounter, people we meet, and paths we walk throughout life. Our reactions to the world are determined by the state of mind we bring to it.

Sometimes when conflicts are raging within us, we needlessly take them outside. Often the "enemy" is not on the other side; it is inside. When we conquer our inner battles, we attain peace within, which we can then bring into the world. When battles continue to rage inside, we live with an imbalanced mind and an out-of-balance life. This happens not just in minds that go out and commit physical violence or harm others with their words. Such battles take place in each of us: when we get angry, irritated, or frustrated; when we provide unconstructive criticism; when we hold resistance inside and take it into the world outside.

When we struggle to understand someone else's actions or words, often the best way to better knowing them is more deeply understanding ourselves. By shifting our attention from the "faults" of others to our own thoughts, words, and actions, we enter an arena where we have full control. Instead of trying to understand and change others, we turn toward inner transformation. When we know ourselves better, we can more easily understand others as well.

Once we recognize that our mind is more than our thoughts, we realize we are certainly not embodied by its ever-changing content. When we take control of our mind, we can learn lessons and absorb wisdom. We recognize that while we cannot always control the challenges we face in life, we can choose our responses to them. And our reactions, more than the challenges themselves, determine their impact on us. True inner peace is where we come to rest when storms are raging outside (or inside). When we bring this peace into the world, our battles shift from violence and war to understanding and resolution.

When we don't know how our mind works, it can seem like a dangerous forest we hesitate to walk through. Let's return to the young woman we met at the start of this chapter. As she ended her talk, she described how she has become a leader focused on helping others escape circumstances like hers. After years of struggle and suffering, she discovered a path to a new life. With awareness, perspective, and positive focused energy, she turned her life around. She found a compass.

CHAPTER EIGHT

Taming the 1D Mind

Darkness cannot drive out darkness; only light can do that.
Hate cannot drive out hate; only love can do that.
—Martin Luther King Jr.

Among the many transformations modern humans attempt, weight loss ranks as one of the most common, especially as obesity continues to grow around the world and increases risks for medical conditions, such as diabetes and liver and heart disease. The US weight-loss industry, with its intention of shrinking America's waistline, has managed to maintain significant expansion for itself, sitting at more than $60 billion in 2013.[22] It includes ever-evolving offerings of fad diets, supplements, and books by celebrities, which continue to rotate through best-seller lists.

While innovators in the pharmaceutical, medical device, and technology industries have tried to conquer obesity, most who have treaded into this space agree: we have no blockbuster solutions, and both waistlines and our spending on reducing them continue to bulge.

When we approach weight loss with the 1D mind, we try to combat our survival and hunger instincts. We can feel as if we are fighting a series of internal battles against our impulses. Inner resistance is high. The desire to give up or the temptation to capitulate may be ever present. When we attempt weight loss using the 2D mind and design carrots, sticks, and metrics to track our progress, we stand a higher chance of success.

Yet such strict, restrictive regimens can be challenging to sustain over the long run. For instance, if we ban a food such as ice cream from our diet, the 1D mind may fear deprivation and remind us of the pleasure of eating ice cream, increasing our cravings. This leads to a battle between the 1D and 2D minds. The 1D mind usually wins, because the perceived short-term need for survival reigns supreme, and in that moment, weight loss seems like a long-term intellectual exercise. Thus, one small nighttime transgression can trigger abandonment of diet plans.

Most stories of lasting weight loss and transformation happen in the 3D mind. Weight loss usually does not begin with focusing on food. Starting with food is like directing our attention to the symptoms of the challenge, instead of its root cause. Of course, food choices and healthy eating play an important role in losing weight. But it helps to start by finding the true "faucet" instead of focusing on "mops." This begins with understanding our relationship to food and, more important, to our body.

In a 1D state, food may be perceived to fill emotional survival needs that extend beyond sheer hunger and include comfort, pleasure, warmth, or protection. Or eating becomes about trying to deal with stress, distress, negative feelings, or reactions to past experiences. These may go as far back as childhood and include unprocessed or difficult emotions. We call this emotional eating or can consider it 1D mind eating. When we understand why we eat what we eat and why we overeat, we begin to address the challenge at its root cause. As we shift how we view our body and its well-being, what we eat begins to matter—we want to nourish it and protect it from harm. Here the analytical capabilities of the 2D mind can be helpful in guiding our food choices.

At a Childhood Obesity Summit I attended in early fall 2013, a 17-year-old teenager shared his story of having weighed 275 pounds and then having shed weight through a program that helped him discover the root causes of his overeating: a childhood parental divorce, stress associated with bullying, and low self-esteem. Focusing on himself as a whole individual, rather than on the labels of his weight struggle, transformed his relationship with food. He said, "You either think of food as your best friend or you hate food, but you have a relationship with it regardless. When you forget about it as a friend or foe and you think about it as one of the three things you need for sustainability—food, shelter, water—it doesn't become a problem. It's manageable."[23]

By not obsessing about food, eating healthy meals, and incorporating exercise into his lifestyle, without keeping track of specific numbers, he lost weight and became healthier. Essentially, he brought awareness into his 1D mind. This allowed him to shift from identifying with the problem to solving it. When transformation began inside, at the origins, there was acceptance. Then even significant lifestyle changes faced less resistance.

The lessons from this story apply to addressing other weaknesses of the 1D mind, such as fear, phobias, addiction, anger, and many other mental health issues. While finding root causes this way may seem more tedious in the short term and takes longer than popping pills, it is often the only lasting solution and saves significant time and resources in the long run. Once we tap into the 3D mind, transformation faces less resistance, feels "right," and is more peaceful, natural, and lasting.

Awareness

When we don't even know what is going on in our mind, we struggle or capitulate. When we know we are dealing with the 1D mind, we can switch from being in it to becoming its observer. Awareness shifts us from identifying with an emotion ("I am angry" or "I am depressed") to recognizing it as a temporary state within us ("Anger or depression is passing through me"). Such a simple change in thinking creates dramatic effects. The power of taming the 1D mind is that just becoming aware of it introduces a pause that begins to calm it down. When we know it cannot harm us, it loses its ability to instill fear and ceases to intimidate us.

Awareness also turns on an inner detector that alerts us to a basic sense of the state of our body—like an internal speedometer. When we know how our body reacts to stress, we can use awareness to counteract its effects before stress takes a stronghold within us. We can become better drivers of our mind. The stress response causes us to step on the gas pedal, and awareness guides us to take our foot off it. Once we learn to read our "speed," we can reduce it anytime. At lower speeds, we can change directions and avoid accidents more easily. The 1D mind can lead us to become stressed, cranky, and aggressive drivers. It is risky to drive either our cars or our lives in a weakened mental state. Then it helps to slow down, pull over, and take a rest, rather than risk crashing. When we move out of the 1D mind we become more relaxed, maintain perspective, and realize we will arrive at our destination regardless of how fast we drive, so we might as well enjoy the ride.

Just like disciplining a child, taming the 1D mind requires compassion. Unlike the 2D mind, it is not convinced by logic and reason. The 1D mind tends to do what it likes and resists strict rules, "sticks," or any other forms of discipline. It perceives restraints as preventing it from satisfying its impulses when, where, and how it wants. Persistently battling urges requires significant mental effort and can become exhausting after a while, causing us to capitulate to the 1D mind. When the 1D mind is "throwing a tantrum," it can be harder to control. Most of us can relate to the experience of saying or doing something in a moment of impulse that we later regret. That regret emerges from awareness, as the 2D and 3D minds recognize—and apologize for—the 1D mind.

We have to teach the 1D mind with patience and love and find simple ways of guiding it from wrong to right, bad to good, and fear to courage. When we embrace it, we earn its trust and can then teach it more easily. When we instill fear or bring anger, resistance grows, leading to struggles and ineffectiveness.

To overcome the 1D mind's weaknesses, it helps not to wrestle or fight them but to acknowledge our feelings, emotions, and experiences. Sometimes this might entail just throwing up our hands and saying, "I surrender." Surrender is not giving up. It is giving up resistance. In a state of resistance, we swim against the currents of our life. By relinquishing the control our emotions and experiences hold over us, we cease to resent or reject our circumstances, our lives, and our selves. When we acknowledge them and then learn to let go, we unleash a powerful cascade.

Once we release what we don't like or want, we obtain the mental space to move toward what we do like or want. When we hold on to pain, it's harder to find paths to healing. In a state of tension, we hold our muscles tight. When we let go, we relax. We cannot both hold on tight and relax. A tense mind focuses only on what is in front of it. A relaxed mind feels safe to wander, explore, and peek around corners.

∾

As individuals and as a society, when we become open to facing challenges and having conversations about them, we gain the courage to overcome them. For instance, if we are battling an inner "tiger" (such as negative feelings, prejudice, judgment, or resentment) with awareness, we can become an observer of our thoughts and actions to understand them better. It is like letting the tiger out in an enclosure where we can study and train it, instead of releasing it during a fight or crisis when it runs wild and can attack us and hurt others.

Most coaching and therapy is designed to introduce awareness to help us gain new perspectives on our circumstances and ourselves. For instance, cognitive behavioral therapy, which can be effective in addressing addictions, phobias, depression, and anxiety, focuses on creating shifts in the mind that enable us to confront the weaknesses of our 1D mind.

Most business and management books, consultants, and executive coaches play the same role. They are "therapy" for companies. They help leaders and managers distance themselves from challenges to confront them more objectively and creatively. Good coaches, counselors, healers, therapists, and leaders don't just tell us what to do—they guide us to finding our own answers and truths so that we can become our own coaches and therapists for life. As we increase our awareness, we recognize our weaknesses and see how they hold us back. We also discover our strengths and how they can move us ahead. And we become better at detecting self-awareness levels in others.

With awareness we can begin to "read" the quality of our thoughts. Like watching weather patterns in the sky, we observe whether they are cloudy and gray or bring rays of sunshine. As soon as we see clouds, or negative thoughts, approaching, we can remove them. How? The simplest way to taming the 1D mind is being positive: thinking positive thoughts, speaking positive words, and engaging in positive actions.

Being Positive

In August 2014, while researching the effects of sleep on well-being I came across a fascinating finding. In 2010, the American Academy of Sleep Medicine (AASM) published a *Best Practice Guide* for the treatment of nightmares. Affecting an estimated 4 percent of the US population and up to 80 percent of PTSD sufferers, nightmare disorder is characterized by recurring, disturbing dreams that evoke negative feelings such as fear, anxiety, or distress and lead to insomnia and fatigue.[24] Described another way, these are negative side effects of the 1D mind.

The AASM *Best Practice Guide* resulted from a detailed review of 57 evidence-based scientific publications covering 29 different treatments, including 18 medical drugs and 11 nondrug therapies. Of the 29 potential treatments for nightmare disorder, only two received the highest recommendation: a pharmaceutical drug and a behavioral therapy known as image rehearsal therapy (IRT).

IRT "utilizes recalling the nightmare, writing it down, changing the theme, story line, ending, or any part of the dream to a more positive one, and rehearsing the rewritten dream scenario so that the patient can displace the unwanted content when the dream recurs."[25]

That's it. "Practiced for 10–20 minutes per day while awake," this simple trick begins to change the mind's nighttime programming. IRT is available for free and easy to use and has no side effects. Just like the placebo effect, it demonstrates the powerful role of our mind in enhancing our well-being. In fact, far beyond curing nightmares, positive thoughts and expectations can have an equally profound effect on our wakeful thoughts.

Why is being positive the most reliable, simple, and effective way out of the 1D mind? The 1D mind tends to default to negative thoughts and reactions because it seeks our survival and is constantly on alert for what can go wrong. Fed by anxiety and fear, it generates countless such scenarios. Requiring little effort and flowing freely, negative thoughts appear much more easily than positive ones.

Yet beyond ensuring our survival, negativity makes us closed-minded, often traps us in rigid thinking patterns, and leaves us reluctant to consider new possibilities. It is a limited-capacity mind, because it defaults to the realm of our past experiences and emotions. It can be easier to think of countless reasons to fear something than to muster the courage to face it. It is often easier to worry incessantly than to stop thinking. To the 1D mind it feels safer to doubt, judge, and remain cynical than to open up and risk vulnerability.

A negative mind operates from a position of seeking familiarity. When faced with anything that poses a risk it says, *Not now!* when it should be asking, *How?* Such pessimism can sometimes be viewed as deeper and more urgent. The 2D mind may dismiss an optimist as a naive simpleton or rationalize negativity as more realistic. Yet negativity holds immense potential for a downward mental spiral. It's a misery-inducing state of mind.

Negative thoughts have a significant herd mentality. One fearful thought arises, the survival instinct activates, and before we know it, an army of negative thoughts marches through our mind. We become paralyzed by fear, diverting focus away from the actions that could lead to positive outcomes. Success becomes more difficult to attain. Negativity also manufactures its own trap, which can manifest in extreme cases as depression. When we lose hope, we cannot see a way out of a problem. Or is it the other way around?

When we think, utter, or act on negative thoughts, regardless of where they are directed, their greatest harm is to us. Just as actions have consequences, thoughts do too. Fear-driven negative predictions of outcomes can drive us to self-sabotaging behaviors. We start identifying with our weaknesses: *I am not good enough* or *I am a failure* and behave in ways that help turn those thoughts into reality. Such thoughts become self-fulfilling, because they seep into our words and actions. Our ability to exit this vicious cycle of the 1D mind is one of the greatest contributors to the difference between failure and success.

We know negative thoughts and expectations can make us sick, as the nocebo effect shows. Anticipating negative outcomes creates a vicious cycle of harm by further putting the body in survival mode. Most of us can relate to the experience of having had pain somewhere in the body that seemed to get worse the more we focused on it and disappeared once we were distracted or became immersed in something else. Sometimes such pain is manufactured by worried, anxious, or negative thoughts. When we inadvertently switch such thoughts off, the pain disappears.

A positive mind is unbelievably powerful. By thinking positive thoughts, we become energized and gain confidence and courage. Positivity opens and expands the mind: it elevates the quality of our thoughts, makes us feel better, and invites ideas that a negative, survival-driven mind simply cannot conceive. A positive mind cannot just *hold* compassion and love; it gives them generously and, in doing so, feels enriched. It expands both our hearts and our minds.

The 1D mind is both our fiercest protector and the greatest barrier to progress in life. When we are in it, we think that its negative thoughts and reactions are a permanent part of us. As the stronghold of the 1D mind is weakened, we realize that thoughts, feelings, emotions, and even experiences are like clouds or storms passing through our skies.

And unlike the weather, we can stave off these storms. We just need to remember that even when we cannot see it, the sun is always there behind the clouds.

Harnessing Positivity

The act of switching from being negative to being positive is based on the simple principle that virtually every negative thought has an antidote: a positive thought at best, a less negative one at worst. For instance, saying, "I hate X" comes from a 1D mind. "X" can stand for a person, a product, a place, or anything else we are capable of loving or hating. The 2D mind can be more rational and say, "I dislike X's trait, action, or behavior," shifting from generalized emotions to the particulars of X that displease us. The 3D mind might say, "I want to understand X," thus approaching X with an open mind.

We can practice generating positive antidotes to negative thoughts moment by moment, thought by thought, knowing that with each switch we attain a more open and powerful mind. Positive thinking is one of the most potent "pills" we can give our mind anytime, anywhere. Antidotes are like affirmations: positive statements about ourselves that create positive emotions, which emit positive energy, and make us feel good within.

Thus with each new thought we create, we have a choice: whether to swallow another bitter pill or switch to its sweet antidote. We can practice this right here and now: Generate a negative thought about yourself and then imagine its exact opposite. For instance, replace "I cannot do this" with "I can do this," or "I am bad/deficient/weak" with "I am good/

sufficient/strong." Positive thoughts may initially require more effort to generate, because they have to overcome the resistance of the 1D mind. Or they may at first ring hollow, because their negative counterparts have held deeply etched, long-standing dominance for years.

Our mind can become so used to a way of thinking that it becomes our truth, and *the* truth for us. We become convinced of our beliefs and ways of looking at the world. Yet by remaining open to new ideas or experiences, we can transform how we see the world. An open mind is willing to consider a story about us that is different from the one we have believed all our lives. It is more agile, resilient, and confident.

With practice, we can produce positive antidotes as easily as negative thoughts and generate more and more of them to dilute and diminish negative thinking. The practice of gratitude also exemplifies this: rather than focusing on what is wrong in our lives, it encourages us to celebrate and cherish what is right. With increased practice, we become better at this negative-to-positive switching process and can use it anytime to shift how we view others, our communities, and the world.

Wellcare meaningfully applies positive affirmations to help healing and recovery. The effects are transformational for those who experience them. Positive affirmations and visualization tap into our inner energy and help us feel better, thus encouraging a relaxed state of being and promoting healing. Several research studies show that being positive can reduce our tendency to get sick, and enhance our ability to recover, heal, and remain healthy. Recent studies on neu-roplasticity, epigenetics, and telomeres suggest that positive thinking may even foster positive changes at the level of our neurons and genes. It may thus reshape our brain and body and extend our life span.

A good friend of mine who had a major organ transplant years ago described over lunch one day how she had returned to work shortly after a surgery. "How did you get back on your feet so quickly after such a major procedure?" I asked. She told me that when she asked her surgeon about this, he said her fierce will to live and determination to get back to work as soon as possible played a role. "You wanted to get well," he said.

This is not just her story. Many doctors and surgeons say that patients with a positive mindset and an inner fire to recover appear to fare better than patients whose maladies might be less severe but who feel hopeless. Of course, often, despite our best intentions, we succumb to disease. But as the placebo effect shows, regardless of our state of health, positive thoughts can supplement and enhance our well-being, no matter what our condition, because they hold the promise of benefit and pose no risk of harm.

~

Positive thinking is a state of flowing with the currents of life, such as driving a car with the flow of traffic. Negative thinking is like going against it—a counterproductive and dangerous undertaking. Learning how to "drive" our mind takes practice. Yet over time, by driving our own mind better, we improve the roads for everyone. As we become more positive, we also become more aware of other people's mental states. We notice how positive, constructive comments in conversations or meetings move discussions forward and how gratuitous negative thoughts, critiques, judgments, and cynicism have the opposite effect.

Being positive doesn't mean we avoid discussing potential risks, conflicts, and downsides related to challenges. It means we do so with a positive intention and a constructive outcome in mind. Instead of focusing on why an initiative, a company, or a strategy will flop, or why a movie, a restaurant, or a book fails to meet our expectations, we maintain an open mind, consider the good intentions of those who poured their blood, sweat, and tears into these creations, and consider what we can do to help them improve.

A positive mind is one of the most contagious human phenomena on Earth. We seek the presence of positive people because their positivity enhances ours. Countless studies and stories reveal how optimists attain greater success in work, life, and the world. People hire and desire positive minds. We are drawn to inspirational leaders. We love to be motivated and moved.

Awareness and positivity take no extra time to implement but transform how we use our mind. The sooner we apply them in our lives, the more days we can enjoy in a state of contentment and peace, no matter what challenges life presents. And when we combine them with perspective and focus, which we explore next, we begin to truly unleash our mind's potential.

Chapter Nine

Training the 2D Mind

Truth is not always art; art is not always truth; but
truth and art have points of contact, which I am seeking.
—Jules Renard

The experience of exploring art with an artist, wine with a vintner, or music with a musician is a journey of magical seduction. We don't just look at a painting of a woman from centuries ago, savor a sip, or listen to a melody. We feel as if we have gazed into Mona Lisa's eyes, perhaps even glimpsed her blink. Vineyard grapes take us on a stroll through rolling fruit orchards and autumn woods. Sweet and seductive tunes carry us into the beat of a musician's soul, a journey in which we often discover our own.

In late spring 2013, I was swept away on such an adventure in, of all places, a local suburban shopping mall. A young friend was visiting after her first year at law school, and we wandered into the fragrances section of a cosmetics store. Standing before the vast array of alluring bottles, which can be as beguiling and delightful as their contents, she offered a few suggestions. As I picked up the samplers to spritz and delight in the perfumes, the "nose" by my side (as experts in perfumery are called) took me on a sweet-scented journey of a lifetime.

What I thought smelled "nice," she revealed as bouquets of roses, garlands of jasmine, citrus orchards, and sandalwood incense. "Do you smell the bergamot and vanilla?" she asked, beckoning me to bring more sense into my sense of scent. She described how the scents would unfold: first, I would smell citrus; moments later, lily of the valley and then musk would appear. The nuanced wonders revealed by her nose I kept hastily verifying against the faint fine print on the perfume bottles and their boxes.

For hours we wandered through the springtime valleys of France, fresh morning bouquets in flower shops, moss-covered woods, and imaginary legends of love lost and found. Decades into life, I felt as if I had just met my nose for the first time. And in the most unexpected way, I learned the power of perspective. I had walked into stores hundreds of times and often paused to smell the perfumes, but this visit was not a hurried survey of scents. We were immersed in them—feeling their meaning, sensing their seductive power. For those few hours, time stood still and we were lost in another world.

Perspective

Just as awareness takes us out of the 1D mind, perspective lifts us beyond the 2D mind. The 2D mind tends to look at the world in practical, measurable, and tangible ways. With perspective our view shifts, exposing us to a bigger picture and new dimensions—we consider the world through different lenses and sometimes remove the lens altogether. We realize some distance from both our thoughts and our ego. Perspective reminds us that, although thinking is one of the mind's primary activities, it does not exist just to think.

Perspective helps us discover the root causes of challenges, rather than rushing to superficial solutions or fleeting fixes that might let a problem fester until it comes back to haunt us, often in worse form than before. We learn to observe both sides and even several different aspects of an issue. Instead of focusing on our own point of view, we seek a common vision, shared goals, and win-win outcomes that leave both sides better off. With perspective, we don't just temporarily solve a conflict or problem—we resolve it.

Perspective also leads us to better decision-making. Decisions define our lives: *Should I take this job? Marry this person? Move to another city? Take a chance? Make a change?* When we consider such decisions through the 1D mind, we tend to see situations as zero-sum games. We perceive potential gains weighed against losses and see options through a self-preservation lens.

By engaging the 2D mind, we gather additional information to help us decide. But sometimes even then we just end up confused. We might decide to go one way but then the 2D mind interrupts to ask, *Well, have you considered it the other way?* We then bounce back and forth between two sides, engaging in binary thinking. The "right" answer is buried in the analysis, but the 2D mind can lead us to indecision and mental paralysis. It doesn't help that the 2D mind is a master rationalizer and can often justify either choice to us.

Yet most of life's big decisions are not driven purely by reason and analysis. In fact, they are often grounded in a deeper sense that one side or the other "feels right." That feeling emerges from the 3D mind and with the benefit of perspective. When we zoom out of the details of a dilemma, we see both sides as part of a greater whole. We view ourselves in the context of a much grander tapestry of humanity. While the 2D mind tries to arrive at *the* right answer, the wisdom of the 3D mind trusts that being open to many answers will guide us to the right one. We attain greater confidence and clarity, and even if doubts appear, we can see a way through them.

~

While the 2D mind creates our place in society, it can be incredibly liberating to be free of it. Perspective distances us from the outcomes of our work, victories, and losses, and reminds us that beyond our successes, achievements, and failures in the world, we are simply human. This may explain why famous men and women at times long for immersion in common, everyday experiences that allow them to forget their fame, which is identification with their ego, and to just have ordinary human experiences.

When we solely define ourselves by our biographies and résumés, our ego overshadows who we truly are. We become known by, and matter because of, what we have and what we have done—how we are known externally. This can introduce separation and lead to arrogance, a sense of superiority, and self-righteousness. It can also amplify fear of failure, in that failure becomes a downfall of the ego and leads to an exaggerated diminution of self-worth, since we have far to fall from a falsely elevated pedestal. When we are not tied to the ever-changing vagaries of our ego, we can move out of our "comfort" zone. We realize that life is filled with trade-offs, and that for almost everything we lose in life, we end up gaining something else. In this way, perspective leads us toward our highest potential. We become the means to a grander vision and discover our true purpose.

Humility is living life with deep perspective. When asked about her lifetime dedication to charitable work with the poorest of the poor in India, Mother Teresa once said, "I don't claim anything of the work. It is his work. I am like a little pencil in his hand. That is all."[26] Many of history's greatest artists, leaders, inventors, and healers held similar philosophies and expressed their work as a higher force working through them. Truly humble people recognize that their achievements are part of the greater arc of humanity. Gandhi, speaking of his work, once said, "I know my own limitations. I am but a humble seeker after truth."[27]

In fact, the teachings of many of the world's spiritual traditions appear to be designed to introduce such perspective into our lives. When we see ourselves as small compared with a larger force—the universe, nature, god, or a deity—we sense our relative insignificance. The more we seek perspective in life, the easier it becomes to attain, until it becomes second nature. We see ourselves as a medium for our mission and give our best to the work that leads to it. We engage in the world out of a deeper connection to our 3D mind.

My friend who guided me through the perfume section had lost her sight in childhood, to the vagaries of the genetic lottery. Yet what her failed eyes might have taken away, the other senses returned, with a depth of insight and imagination that most who continuously look at the world often fail to see. Her beautiful mind is the embodiment of perspective, and her ways of looking at the world perpetually broaden mine.

What creates such minds? I realized that nurturing perspective allowed her to attain immense focus. She turned a potential weakness into her strength by focusing on all of her other senses and making the most of her mind. This led her to attend both a leading college and a top law school.

Before our journey continues, to offer you a glimpse of her spirit, I will leave you with a few of her words, which she once wrote in a review of her favorite perfume: "It reminded me of lemon orchards and laundry hanging out to dry under a cerulean sky, of white flowers strewn all over a Mediterranean beach, of water and wind dancing an ancient waltz at the edge of the world. It was the smell of sunshine mingling with the foam-tipped waves of the ocean. I was besotted and am still am."

Focus

Focus is committing our presence, intentions, and energy to what matters most. It is a concentration of thought and action that brings clarity to life and creates momentum for attaining our goals. Focus helps us transform failure to success by recognizing challenges as temporary setbacks, not permanent destinations. Just as awareness and positivity amplify each other, our abilities to attain perspective and gain focus fuel each other.

With focus, we can zoom into life to bring positive attention to what matters and eliminate what does not. We reduce noise, clutter, and distractions in our mind. What is mental clutter? Rethinking a past, which cannot be changed, worrying about a future that we have little control over, or ruminating about what is going on in another person's mind. It is the churning thought factory of the 2D mind. When we think indiscriminately, our thoughts become diluted.

Focus trains the 2D mind and prevents it from continually jumping from one thought to the next and tiring itself to exhaustion. With focus we can harness powerful, positive thoughts, instead of getting distracted by weak, negative ones. It shifts our attention from ruminating about the past and worrying about the future to living in the present. We relinquish thoughts that are not helpful to our life, such as old ideas, grudges, resentment, and outdated notions.

We can also use focus to shift our attention from the minds of others to our own. When we concentrate on the present moment and on our self, we behold the two factors we have the greatest control over changing at any time. Even if the change is just a new reaction to an old problem, we can try it out immediately. In this way, focus becomes a powerful catalyst for transformation.

An important aspect of focus is being able to say no. Usually it is easier to say no to something we don't want than to something that looks good enough. Fear creeps in and asks, *What if nothing better comes along?* Yet to attain the "great," sometimes we have to say no to many "good enoughs." To explore this, consider a task you would like to get done, and then, on a scale of 1 to 10, decide how important it is to you. A task ranked 10 is absolutely critical (e.g., eating or sleeping). We tend to prioritize such tasks because our survival depends on them. When we create a goal but rank it much below 10 (e.g., finding a dream career, improving work-life balance, resolving a long-standing conflict), excuses and distractions derail us. Under the auspices of the 1D mind, obstacles turn into reasons to quit prematurely or to justify failure.

A low-priority goal is not set up for success and can become counterproductive. It takes up our mindshare but often doesn't gain enough inner momentum to cross the finish line. Such goals can even dilute and distract our focus from our most important ones, reducing our chances for success in all of them.

Thus, when we decide that a goal deserves only our half-hearted effort, we should carefully consider whether it is worth our time at all. Here, "no" can be a positive, aligning force. What to let go of and eliminate can be harder to figure out, but often it matters as much as what we focus on. By identifying the former, we come closer to attaining the latter. Removing distractions brings freedom and prevents derailment from our paths. Less truly becomes more.

Less Is More

This principle is the secret power of simplicity. To distill something to its simplest essence requires more thoughtfulness than just dwelling in its messy convolutions. Thus true simplicity is much deeper than complexity, because it integrates perspective on what matters. Focus and simplicity are intertwined and each begets the other. Great minds through the ages have had a gift for extracting simplicity from complexity and for discovering pearls of wisdom in life's challenges.

Rainer Maria Rilke's famous *Letters to a Young Poet* emerged from such depth of thought, distilling wisdom on creating art into timeless advice that continues to guide us, long after both poets have passed away. As Rilke once wrote, "Works of art are of an infinite solitude, and no means of approach is so useless as criticism. Only love can touch and hold them and be fair to them."[28] Rilke reminds us of the fundamental source of art, which also holds the essence of how to approach it. He continues, "Being an artist means: not numbering and counting, but ripening like a tree, which doesn't force its sap, and stands confidently in the storms of spring, not afraid that afterward summer may not come. It does come."[29]

Rilke also acknowledges that such wisdom emerges from the depths of our inner being: "Don't think that the person who is trying to comfort you now lives untroubled among the simple and quiet words that sometimes give you pleasure. His life has much trouble and sadness, and remains far behind yours. If it were otherwise, he would never have been able to find those words."[30] Rilke's beautiful letters continue to "comfort" and guide generations of artists on how to stay true to their art.

Focus is also one of the most consistent differentiating factors contributing to creativity. Great artists and musicians say they live and breathe their art. Many writers, when asked about their work, say they are always "writing." Even when shopping, walking, or sitting in a coffee shop, they observe, notice, and ponder the world around them. It is the same with many inventors and innovators. This explains the power of our vocation and avocation being the same: we think about what we enjoy, and it happens to be our day's work too—so we focus much of our time on it.

One way of fostering simplicity in our minds is by bringing it into our physical lives. Simplicity does not mean that we eliminate the variety that adds spice to life. It means that we bring simplicity to those dimensions of our life where variety might be distracting and can overwhelm or exhaust us, leading to stress. Mental clutter and physical clutter can become part of a vicious cycle, in which each feeds the other. When we simplify our environment, we begin to observe how our mind becomes calmer.

For instance, we can examine each of our material possessions through the lens of two questions: *Is it absolutely necessary?* or *Does it bring me great joy?* What we declutter varies: some simplify their homes and wardrobes, others their social commitments and activities. As we simplify our lives, we often attain more serenity in our minds. It is no coincidence that many of the greatest figures in history also led some of the simplest lives. A less scattered mind gets more done. In our modern, distraction-filled lives, the need for simplicity is greater than ever.

Do or Die

Focus comes into our lives in two ways. Sometimes we proactively cultivate it to attain a goal. At other times life thrusts us into crises that leave us no choice but to focus. Despite the pain they bring, and sometimes because of their associated suffering, crises serve as powerful transformation catalysts. They make us consider, whether we would like to or not, what truly matters to us and why. Crises, such as the death of a loved one or massive personal or professional failure, can take us to the brink and make us confront life at its most fundamental level. Individuals who have lost a parent or faced hardship in childhood often develop coping mechanisms that give them greater focus for the rest of their lives. They take nothing for granted—even life.

A crisis is often a forced stripping away of what holds us back. In being forced to face ourselves we break open the countless little boxes within which we have been comfortable thinking. We reevaluate all our prior assumptions. When life explodes, its fragments often end up in unexpected places. Gathering them back up becomes a journey of stepping beyond the familiar. Our life often reassembles in new ways, and, in the process, reveals the building blocks for future success.

Some of the most lucid voices in the world are those of individuals who have stared death, the ultimate crisis, in the face and walked back unafraid. Others are those of people dealing with a chronic, life-threatening illness, who walk on the tightrope of life, aware they can fall off (die) at any moment, yet live each step with an inner richness that those merely walking on solid ground rarely experience. When we stare death in the face, all else becomes irrelevant.

One of the most inspiring speakers I have heard in recent years is an opera singer who underwent a double lung transplant—twice. And she continues to sing. At a talk I attended in 2012, she said, "My life is a very literal continuation of the deaths of two other people. Death isn't just something for the sick and the old, and while its sting is real, good can come from it. Death is as much a part of life as love, birth, and happiness."[31] She described how her dance with death gave her a new perspective on life. She spoke with rare depth and lucidity about the beauty of life and love, echoing timeless wisdom, as if from a 3D mind, as she said, "Once we come to peace with our own mortality, we can finally start living lives worth dying for."

Yet we need not wait for crises to initiate change. The process of increasing focus and concentration is like building a muscle. It requires regular exercise—repetitive effort that enhances our strength and endurance. A thought becomes stronger when it is repeated, and that further strengthens our ability to focus on it. Challenges can be like weights in resistance training, accelerating the process.

As we learn how to navigate with this compass for our mind, awareness shows us where we are, and perspective where we would like to be. Being positive and bringing focus into our thoughts and actions then guides us there. As we become stronger, we can lift heavier weights. Then, no matter what our circumstances, we know how to recognize fragments of hope and find our way out.

∼

When we discover awareness and perspective, we find our way to the 3D mind. When we realize some distance from external factors, which are ever changing, we come closer to the serenity that emerges from within. Rather than being at the mercy of the outer world, our state of being becomes a reflection of our inner tranquility. Regardless of what the outside looks like, we find peace within. At this point, your 2D mind might be wondering: If we are each filled with such potential for goodness, why do we continue to bear suffering and sorrow? Why do some of us falter during crises? Why do humans receive and give hurt—to each other and to themselves?

The pain humans project onto the world often represents an inability to confront, bear, and process such pain within. When we feel disconnected within, from our inner energy, we can feel alone, angry, or afraid. The 3D mind retreats, and the 1D mind dominates. An otherwise manageable circumstance is then perceived as a matter of do-or-die self-preservation. When inner torment, suffering, and hurt struggle to find a safe, protective place to resolve themselves, they continue to grow like a cancer that can eventually consume its host. Everything—even our life itself—can look like a threat and can lead us to hopelessness and despair, or worse, to violence and vengeance. The pain within lashes out. This is the root cause of most evil in the world.

Yet there is no duality between good and evil or peace and war. Those are constructs of the 2D mind. The destructive aspects represent encounters with the dark side of human nature in our 1D mind. War is just a roadblock on the path to peace. The potential for goodness and peace is within each of us. We can each find our way there—regardless of who we are and what our journeys on Earth have been. Positive focused energy shows us the way.

CHAPTER TEN

Trusting the 3D Mind

Behind all seen things lies something vaster; everything is but a path,
a portal, or a window opening on something other than itself.
—Antoine de Saint-Exupéry

Sometimes we travel to new places to explore new worlds. At other times, in old places, we discover the world anew. In March 2013, I journeyed with my mother to Varanasi, India, one of the oldest continuously inhabited cities on Earth and the cradle of her childhood memories.

To this day, Varanasi is a magical, mystical place, and walking through its maze of narrow alleys is akin to entering the pages of history. Here and in other such cradles of civilization—Jerusalem, Rome, and Athens—vivid tales from tour guides roll through the air, echoing ancient voices that gain new life in each retelling and beckon us to remember their oft-forgotten wisdom.

One marked contrast between this ancient city and its counterparts in the Western world is that walking through Varanasi is not for the faint of heart (or nose). Cows are holy here and have the right of way. They seem to know it well, because in many alleys no wider than their length, they are the most frequent cause of traffic jams. Humans scurrying through the alleys might be in a hurry, but the cows, they always take their time. Perhaps they are wiser that way. Yet cows drop dung, which mixes with plastic bags, disposable plates, and food waste among a veritable zoo of dogs, crows, monkeys, and rats that inhabit the same narrow alleys as humans do, knowing well the virtues of such a rich habitat.

Strolling through the alleys of Varanasi, I realized that when life becomes so concentrated in a place, and tied into such deep coexistence with other forms of life, a new order emerges. All living beings pass through these narrow walkways with a sense of harmony—an understanding that we depend on, and need each other. As an old man sitting outside his home said to me, when people have little, they focus their lives on the things that money cannot buy anyway—looking out for each other, expressing gratitude for life, and seeing each life, however desperate or dejected its circumstances, as a precious gift deserving dignity. More than once, I saw one gaunt beggar reach out to another to share a meager meal.

Here in Varanasi, life and death stroll hand in hand, like natural companions through the ages. Families carrying their departed beloved crisscross the same alleys where city life pulsates and tourists walk. The living, the dying, and the dead intermingle so naturally that transitions from one to the next begin to feel as rhythmic as the rising and setting of the sun.

Perhaps this is why, while the sun often rises unnoticed among the hurried lives of high-rise cities, it does not simply rise in Varanasi. In this city on the ancient banks of the river Ganges, the sun is welcomed each dawn with festive songs, prayers, and flower offerings. Each morning, as I saw its first glimmers glow behind the fields on the opposite bank, I sensed more than a new day, a new beginning—a renewed celebration of life. Gathered on the banks of the river are people of all ages, drinking chai, singing songs, and taking their morning bath while basking in the sun's precious first glowing rays. In the distance, smoke rises from cremation pyres, where the fire is said to have been burning continuously for the last few thousand years.

In this place that spans ancient and modern, life and death, and despair and hope, I realized that life, at its best and worst, is an exploration—a journey in search of meaning. And such meaning can be discovered anywhere, when we pause to experience it.

How often do we stop to fully experience the sun's rising and setting over the varied majestic horizons of the earth? It will rise again tomorrow. The question is, will you be there to witness it—not just the literal rising of the sun but also the part of it within your being? For just like the sun that ascends each dawn, a force within us rises every moment of our lives. When we pause to experience it, we cease to just live and become alive. That force is our inner energy.

Positive Focused Energy

Our journey to learning to first experience and then trust the 3D mind begins with awareness. As we become aware of ourselves and that we are more than our thoughts, we gain perspective. By being positive, we tame the 1D mind and release its control over us. With focus we can free ourselves from the tyranny of our ego and the activities of our 2D mind. We come to recognize that there is more to our life than surviving and thinking. Yet then we begin to wonder: Who are we beyond our thoughts? Do we matter at that level? How do we know?

One morning during my trip to Varanasi, while observing the sun's first rays, I became acutely aware of the world around me and within me. I smelled the incense from the prayer mats, heard temple bells ringing in the distance, felt the soft flower petals in my palms, delighted in the taste of warm chai from a clay cup, and witnessed the sun's awakening. Lost in this experience, I forgot myself. Then deep perspective emerged. It dawned on me that beyond our physically visible and intellectually manifested lives, there is an energy—a sensation of an experience—that both transcends our mind and imparts meaning to it. It is a sense of belonging to something greater than our selves that brings a deep sense of harmony, contentment, and meaning.

We realize that who we truly are, at our deepest essence, extends far beyond the superficial and surface-level ways in which we define, label, and divide our world. This inner energy has a universal quality whenever it lifts us into the 3D mind: it is positive focused energy.

$\sim$

Positive focused energy is the source of our creative and innovative potential and leads us to our intuition and wisdom. It is at the heart of an innovator's breakthrough, an entrepreneur's success, and a leader's impact. It is present in an artist's brushstroke and in a writer's voice. It is also there when music lifts us, when we speak our truths, and when deep clarity emerges. It is the source of a doctor's compassion and a force in many patients' healing. Experiencing this energy breathes life into places, love into people, and meaning into experiences. It turns a daily sunrise in an old city into enduring inspiration. It enlightens our most meaningful moments. It is the current flowing through us when we feel truly alive and is the lifeblood of love and connection. Once our basic needs are met, it is what humanity hungers for in virtually everything we do.

We seek it through joyful experiences, loving relationships, or work that imbues us with a feeling of meaning. Genuine charisma, confidence, and chemistry also arise from positive focused energy. Sometimes when two new people meet, they sense an immediate connection, as if they have found a dear old friend. We call this chemistry, since it transcends the usual bounds of human interaction. This happens because both people experience a connection with their inner energy and help generate positive focused energy in each other.

Why is positive focused energy so powerful? Because it is the most simple, direct, and easy way to simultaneously tame the 1D mind, train the 2D mind, and learn to trust the 3D mind. When we are positive, we relinquish fear, reduce stress, and become more aware of ourselves. When we are focused, we can stop our mind from running all over the place. We also reduce the ego's grip over us. When we have positive focused energy within us, we access the 3D mind. In this way, the 3D mind and positive focused energy beget each other.

Harnessing Energy

Unlike the body and mind, which we can attempt to study through science, most of us go through life with minimal understanding of our inner energy levels and the reasons for their fluctuations. Sometimes we feel that we have high energy and at other times low energy. In fact, we can go from experiencing high energy to feeling low energy in a short window of time.

When we are having a stressful day, our body may not be working any harder than on other days. But stress, worry, and negative thinking drain us of energy and leave us feeling physically exhausted. The reverse is also true—positive thoughts elevate us, and we can often feel energized in particular places or in the presence of passionate and inspirational friends, colleagues, family members, leaders, and speakers.

Throughout life, we tend to exist in a few basic energy states. Once we recognize these, we can engage in activities that harness positive focused energy:

1. *Lazy*: When we are feeling lethargic, dull, depressed, tired, or as if we are stuck in a rut, it is often because we have gotten trapped in the 1D mind and are disconnected from the 3D mind. Then firing up our energy levels begins with thinking, saying, or engaging in something positive or uplifting to energize us.

2. *Edgy*: When we are feeling anxious or agitated, we have high energy but it can feel stressful, scatter our attention, and exhaust us. In this state, we are trapped in the 1D

and 2D minds. Restlessness is negative, scattered energy. We can reduce its power over us by immersing ourselves in an activity that brings serenity, meaning, and joy. By giving our thoughts a positive anchor, and by focusing on what brings us contentment, we help our mind relax.

3.   *Lively*: This is an excited state—one of positive energy. We are happy and feel energized. This state taps into the strengths of the 1D and 2D minds. It is the source of much of our daily productivity and helps us get things done, because we are operating from a position of guiding the 1D and 2D minds, instead of being controlled by them. When we bring focus to such energy, we harness our highest potential.

4.   *Serene*: This state reflects positive focused energy. We are filled with positivity and focus while maintaining a sense of peace and contentment. We often arrive at this state in solitude or while immersed in activities in which we lose our identification with the 1D and 2D minds. This state is known by many names: athletes call it being in the "zone," artists and musicians describe it as a sense of "flow," and meditation practitioners experience it in their quietest moments.

The lazy state is low energy. Both the edgy and lively states can leave us feeling tired after a while. But when we are in a serene state, we build up energy. It feels rejuvenating and energizes us. By becoming aware of these states, we begin to recognize which experiences lift us, and which ones leave us feeling drained. Then we can proactively harness our inner energy anytime. Positive focused energy is infectious. Happy people make us happy. If both the giver and the recipient are in a state of positive focused energy, both are lifted higher. Thus, teams with a common vision, mission, and purpose attain remarkable feats. When someone feels negative, scattered, or down, he or she can make others feel drained of energy in his or her presence. Although, if the recipient of such energy remembers the power of awareness, perspective, and positive focused energy, he or she can use them as "immunizations."

Thinking positive thoughts energizes us. Saying "I am" brings energy to words. When we speak positive words, like "I am happy," we are uplifted. When we speak negative ones, like "I am angry," we may, in subtle ways, without even realizing it, dissipate our energy. Most thoughts are conversations we have with ourselves, yet our thoughts have great power. They shape our reality. Our thoughts translate into our words and our actions. We tend to guard our actions more than our words and our words more than our thoughts. Yet when we treat each thought with the seriousness of action and bolster it with positive focused energy, we unlock the power of our mind.

We witness this truth in dramatic detail at sporting events. From Olympic coaches to star athletes, it is well acknowledged that even in a body trained to its highest physical potential, the secret of peak athletic performance is the state of mind an athlete brings to it. We celebrate moments when an athlete overcomes a physical setback to win a game, or when one written off as an underdog trains with seemingly superhuman perseverance to reach the top of his or her sport.

Physical setbacks and weaknesses can be overcome when a body pushed to its limits reaches beyond them, bolstered by the powers of the mind. Such moments symbolize what is possible when we bring our highest physical and mental potential to facing life's challenges. When we believe in ourselves, we give our best to the world and unleash the true power of our mind.

Faith in Energy

While meeting entrepreneurs over the years, I always looked for ones who embodied passion and believed so deeply in their mission that they viewed the risks surrounding their work as surmountable tasks. Passionate entrepreneurs see obstacles as building blocks and setbacks as opportunities. When we are passionate about something, it lights a fire within us. We are filled with a sense of purpose that extends beyond the needs and desires of our 1D and 2D minds.

When our work fuels our passion, we pursue it with confidence. By believing in ourselves and in the mission of our work, we create an easier path to success. By investing our energy in it, we generate more positive focused energy. Work becomes play and feels so compelling that we are willing to give much of ourselves to it. Passion is positive focused energy.

The ability to believe in something that we don't fully understand—to have faith—is necessary to harness our potential. To be able to trust the 3D mind, we need to believe in it. Such faith is an ephemeral aspect of success that is often not discussed. But it is impossible to talk about transformation without understanding how faith fuels and drives so many of us. When our faith is strong, we gain the courage and conviction to conquer fear and doubt.

The most powerful knowledge on faith comes from the world's religions, most of which seem to have started out as guidelines for living a good and righteous life in the context of the times when each was born. At a basic level, religion seeks universal truths—values by which to lead our lives, principles to make sense of our world, and paths that lead to peace. Religion often steps in when other explanations fail: unexpected tragedy, miraculous experiences, unbearable challenges, and the vagaries of human interaction.

Traveling back in time, through words that have survived the centuries, we seem in each epoch to have believed that we were standing at a critical juncture in history. Essentially, humanity has lived through a succession of epic times. The questions we asked centuries ago are the same ones we ponder today. What can we learn from the past? How do we lead good lives? What legacy do we leave our children?

Despite the variety of religions in the world, many people are turned off by religion altogether or turn away from it because they feel constrained by its rituals or rigid beliefs. When religion instills fear, it draws on the 1D mind. When it imposes rituals, it taps into the 2D mind. Yet the ultimate purpose of most religions is to lead us to the same destination—not roughly the same but exactly the same: the 3D mind.

Prayers, songs, and rituals are means to that end and they can help us access our positive focused energy. Consider this metaphor. Today, we have technologies to harness different forms of energy (e.g., hydro, wind, or solar). All have the same intended result—they light the same bulb. In the same way, different faiths offer varied paths to the 3D mind. Some are widespread, others confined to niches. Yet most of the world's major spiritual traditions echo the same universal wisdom. They speak of love, peace, and compassion as powerful uniting forces. I discovered "proof" of this principle at the Library of Congress one day, when I stumbled upon a book on wisdom from the world's living religions. Each of its chapters discussed a different faith and began with a quote from that religion:

1. Hatred is not diminished by hatred at any time. Hatred is diminished by love—this is the eternal law. (Buddhism: *Dhammapada*, 5)

2. A new commandment I give to you, that you love one another. (Christianity: *John* 13:34)

3. Confucius was asked: "Is there one word that sums up the basis of all good conduct?" And he replied, "Is not 'reciprocity' that word? What you yourself do not desire, do not put before others." (Confucianism: *Analects*, XV)

4. True religion is to love, as God loves them, all things, whether great or small. (Hinduism: *Hitopadesa*)

5. All living beings hate pain; therefore one should not injure them or kill them. This is the essence of wisdom: not to kill anything. (Jainism: *Sutra-krit-anga*)

6. Do not unto others that which is hateful to you. This is the whole of the Law; all the rest is commentary. (Judaism: *Rabbi Hillel, Talmud*)

7. No one is a true believer until he loves for his brother what he loves for himself. (Islam: *Hadith*)

8. One should not be mindful of suffering in his own life and unmindful of suffering in the lives of others. (Shintoism: Sacred Text of *Kyo Koyen*)

9. He is fit to govern who loves all people as he loves himself. (Taoism: *Tao-Te King*, 13)

10. On three excellent things be ever intent: good thoughts, good words, and good deeds. (Zoroastrianism: *Vendidad* XVIII, 17)[32]

All utter the same enduring truth: treat each other with love. In essence, the world's spiritual practices lead us to realizing the deepest wisdom of the 3D mind, that at the most fundamental level we are all the same. When we trust and live by this truth, transformation begins.

Positive thoughts and feelings build enduring, creative, and constructive bonds that bridge differences and bring us together at a purely human level. They bring out the best in us and help us bring it out in each other. We sometimes come to believe that an elevated state of being arises within us because of an outside factor—a belief system, a person, or an achievement—or that we attain such a "high" while inspired, victorious, or in love. Yet we can each access this state by harnessing positive focused energy.

Consider our journey through these pages akin to planting a seed—that of our highest potential. This seed is not an occasional gift randomly bestowed on a few of us. It is there within each of us, and it is the same within all of us. It begets kindness, compassion, empathy, love, and peace and is purely positive. Learning to become the gardener of our seed is one of the simplest yet most powerful skills for life, and it represents the most valuable and untapped resource to transform our world. Just as with a seed in nature, this seed has remarkable intelligence within it. Its transformation begins when it meets the soil and receives air, water, and light to undertake a miraculous journey from an unformed speck to a beautiful living form. To guide its growth, our metaphorical seed needs positive (soil), focused (water) energy (sunlight).

If the seed is not growing, usually the defect is not in the seed. It may just lack enough soil, water, or sunlight. We also cannot keep pulling it out to check on its roots. In the same way, constant doubt can weaken us. The growth of a sapling is not apparent in a given minute, but the passage of time reveals its transformation. In the same way, tapping into the 3D mind depends on trust—trusting that it is always there within us and that it holds wisdom for us. When we connect to our inner energy, our wisdom, intuition, and insights flow. Then we access the magic and mystery that bring beauty and meaning to life. Learning to listen to and completely trust the 3D mind is a lifelong journey.

～

Science can tell us how the solar system is organized and that the earth is orbited by a small gray rock that is illuminated by the sun's reflection at night. Yet when you happen to wake up at five in the morning, as I did on a warm August day in 2014, and witness an orange glowing orb sinking into the distant horizon in the dark sky, it is a moment of pure mystery. The moon has guided all our ancestors, regardless of their languages or beliefs, and it has been a silent witness to the entire arc of human history—from our brightest to our darkest moments. We have created countless legends about it, and even now, despite knowing that we have walked its barren terrain, it evokes a sense of wonder and on a silent summer dawn inspires reverence.

Both the sunrise in Varanasi and the moonset in Bethesda reminded me that our limitation in being able to measure our inner energy is utterly unrelated to its power. Life's exquisiteness and elegance are grounded in it. This energy is the source of not just meaning but also the courage to begin transformation and to take on anything that resists change, whether it is old habits or outdated thinking.

When we seek and discover answers within us, clarity emerges. We realize what we are running from and toward in life and why. Then it becomes easier to find paths to where we would like to go. The next section offers a brief rest stop where we learn the "logistics" of traveling from the 1D and 2D minds into the 3D mind. Then our own adventures begin as we create and explore new paths in our minds, our lives, and the world.

IV. Guide

CHAPTER ELEVEN

Many Paths

Our paths may well be different.
If our destination is the same, we shall meet there.
—Mahatma Gandhi

On a chilly late-October afternoon in 2013, I joined a gathering of more than 250 doctors, nutritionists, nurses, and a smattering of curious souls in a nondescript airport-hotel ballroom in northern Virginia, just across the river from Washington, DC. Much less formal than the biotechnology conferences of my earlier years, this remains the only professional convention I have attended where most speakers received cheers, whistles, and standing ovations from their peers.

For three days, the stage was traversed by titans and icons in the emerging field of lifestyle medicine, which seeks to incorporate evidence-based lifestyle practices—primarily diet and exercise—into mainstream medicine to prevent and treat the chronic diseases overwhelming our healthcare system. This impassioned group sought ways to turn off the faucet of disease, rather than resorting to "mops"—pills and procedures—as the first line of defense.

The speaker at the podium that afternoon was a tall, lanky medical doctor in his 60s. He had spent the last 40 years studying the effects of diet in causing and reversing chronic diseases such as diabetes, rheumatoid arthritis, multiple sclerosis, irritable bowel syndrome, and hypertension. During his talk, he built the case for the diet he "prescribed": a vegetarian, whole foods, plant–based (vegetables, grains, beans), high-starch (about 80 percent of daily calories), low-fat (10 percent of calories), low-protein (10 percent of calories), low-fruit, and dairy-free regimen.

He shared more than 30 supporting clinical studies and publications spanning the last century, which supported the idea that his dietary prescription could stabilize, and potentially even reverse, diabetes and reduce blood glucose, cholesterol, and triglyceride levels. He presented more than a dozen patient case studies with "before" and "after" photos illustrating dramatic weight loss and fitter, younger-looking physiques. Some patients had even been weaned off prescription medications. The talk was persuasive—data-driven for an evidence-minded audience, clinically compelling, and eminently feasible.

There was just one problem. Over the course of the conference, speaker after speaker followed the same format—presenting a unique dietary regimen and bolstering it with extensive studies. Some advised eating no animal-based products. Others promoted certain fish as part of a healthy diet. Some advocated healthy unsaturated fats from nuts, seeds, and olive oil. Others insisted on cutting out all fat. While each diet was individually convincing, many were mutually exclusive. This confusion is not unlike that created by daily health-news headlines. Today a headline proclaims coffee is bad for our health, and tomorrow another announces it is good for us. At this conference, most speakers supported low-fat, plant-based, vegetarian diets. Yet in the wider world, other diet gurus advocate eating meat, dairy, and eggs—foods that remain staples in most modern diets. So how do we determine which diet is best for us?

I realized this question extends far beyond what we eat. When we are deciding what is best for us, whether for our body or for our mind, how much should we be guided by data from studies? What is the role of our own experience? How do we decide which data to rely on and which experiences to draw upon, both those of others and our own?

In our "big data" times, it seems we can find "evidence" to support almost anything. We are increasingly sophisticated at generating and analyzing vast volumes of data. Yet our data gathering methods and statistical analyses sometimes become as subjective as the humans they are supposed to guide. So how do we identify practical truths for leading our own lives?

∽

Even after we have this map and compass to explore and navigate our mind, we still need to know how best to harness awareness, perspective, and positive focused energy to travel with ease between our different states of mind. As with most journeys, there are usually many ways to get there from here. The same path can be a superhighway for some and a mule's passage for others. Or we might rely on one mode when we are feeling lazy and a different one when we are feeling edgy.

To find the paths that are best for us, we can take suggestions from others or even rely on guides for exploring options. But no one else can decide our paths for us. We choose our own paths just as we decide what to eat every day: based on our own knowledge and direct experience. Our firsthand experience becomes the lasting guide, revealing answers that others can merely suggest. Once we find paths we call our own, we can walk them all our days.

Paths into the Mind

The process of shifting how our mind works happens in subtle ways. It begins the moment a new idea takes hold in our mind and is reinforced by subsequent ideas and experiences that resonate with it. We can accelerate this process by pursuing activities that proactively take us out of the 1D and 2D minds and into the 3D mind. Such pursuits strengthen our mind's capacity to travel with ease between the three states of mind and help us harness awareness, perspective, and positive focused energy.

A pursuit is an activity in which we happily engage and become immersed. It might be going for a walk, run, swim, or bike ride; or dancing, cooking, gardening, playing a musical instrument, engaging in crafts, or spending time in nature. Some paths into the mind have survived through the ages, and we will explore a few of them here. Each such pursuit engages both our body and our mind to take us out of our routine thinking patterns and to release the hold of the 1D and 2D minds. In addition, to take us into the 3D mind a pursuit needs to allow for alert serenity—moments when our mind is so engrossed in the pursuit that we forget ourselves and the passage of time.

While exploring different pursuits, I looked into modern research on habits. Initially, I was surprised to learn that no single duration ensures success in forming, adopting, and sustaining a habit—not 7 days, nor 21 or 30 days. Then I realized that when a new habit takes hold within us at a deeper level—when it generates positive focused energy and taps into our 3D mind—adopting it becomes easier. Then even just a few days can be enough to begin transformation. When we try to adopt a new habit with just our 1D or 2D mind, even significant effort can leave us frustrated in attempts to change.

For this reason, the activities we choose to pursue need to resonate within. They should bring such levels of meaning, relaxation, enjoyment, and contentment that we look forward to engaging in them. Often this doesn't happen the first few times we try a new pursuit, because we are still in the early stages of learning it. But if such inner feelings don't arise once we get to know a path, it will likely be suboptimal for taking us into the 3D mind. We also need to maintain faith and trust in the paths we walk. If we hold any inner resistance, the 1D and 2D minds will keep disrupting our journey.

To take us out of the 1D mind and its oft-associated stress response, a pursuit should encourage our full immersion in it. Thus, we cannot simultaneously be doing something else—such as using an electronic device. To then also take us out of the 2D mind, a pursuit should not require our continuous, undivided attention. It should enable moments of serenity. Playing a game of tennis can be enjoyable and relaxing and take us out of the 1D mind, but it is challenging to exit the 2D mind when it is continuously focused on the movement of the ball.

When we are learning a new skill or hobby, such as gardening, cooking, or playing an instrument, the 2D mind is fully engaged. Once we attain basic mastery, when a pursuit doesn't require our undivided attention, we begin to gain glimpses of the 3D mind. Such moments appear for a musician while playing an instrument, for an artist while creating art, for a scientist while conducting research, and for a writer while writing.

Comfortable with the basic skills of our craft, we become immersed in peaceful exploration. During such moments, we give the present—the here and now—our undivided attention. We lose track of time and forget ourselves. A deep sense of harmony and connection emerges. This is why many musicians, artists, athletes, and writers find so much meaning, contentment, and fulfillment in their work. Even after hours of immersion, as we tap into positive focused energy and our 3D mind, we feel energized.

Ideally, we each discover a few paths. When we are feeling lazy or lethargic, we can get up and walk, run, play, or just move the body; when we are feeling edgy or restless, we can engage in a relaxing activity. Sometimes we also glimpse the 3D mind while engaged in mundane activities such as washing dishes, walking a dog, commuting to work, or using the bathroom. Hot-shower genius is real—an unhurried shower or bath relaxes our body and soothes our mind, drawing us into the present moment and often into the 3D mind.

Some of us might also gain positive focused energy while reading a book or watching an inspirational film or talk. To truly transform our mind and our life we ultimately need to become more deeply involved—to act, to be on the stage of life, sensing, experiencing, experimenting, and creating—rather than just sitting and spectating.

Sometimes individuals engage in pursuits such as drinking alcohol or smoking with the intention of "relaxing." Yet these activities amplify the 1D mind. While they seem to temporarily erase pain or exhaustion, they usually leave one craving more and can increase anxiety and discontentment over the long run. They rarely lead to lasting contentment and serenity.

Similarly, watching TV, playing video games, or surfing the Internet can provide a temporary sense of unwinding. But these activities don't lead us into the 3D mind because they provide continuous stimuli. The purpose of any path out of the 1D and 2D minds and into the 3D mind is not losing the mind to forget our selves but tapping into the mind to find our true selves.

Here we will explore a few such pursuits. These are by far not the only ones. If you would like to delve into any of these or find others, countless other books and courses can guide you. Just remember your destination: harnessing positive focused energy and tapping into the 3D mind.

Being in Nature

One of the most nourishing activities for the mind is being in nature. Mountains, oceans, rivers, forests, and meadows reconnect us to the essence of life. In touch with its vast and beautiful landscapes, we look at our world at a scale that surpasses human boundaries and definitions. Being in nature is profoundly awe inspiring and it imbues us with both awareness and perspective. We realize that even humanity's most spectacular creations, such as the pyramids, are minuscule compared to nature's majestic history and scale.

Nature's palettes and landscapes relax us and reawaken our senses. Fresh air energizes us. Nature is an enduring source of restoration and renewal both in how it takes care of itself and in what it reveals to us about ourselves. When we give nature our undivided attention, it becomes one of our most powerful paths into the 3D mind.

Creative Expression

Creativity, curiosity, and exploration also encourage and nurture the 3D mind. While formal schooling hones the intellect, our intuition is cultivated by engaging in disciplines such as art, music, dance, and other forms of creative expression.

While science and technology are critical for progress, the liberal arts and humanities play an equally important role. They enrich our inner lives. The arts teach us about meaning and humanity. Continued support and promotion of diverse art forms in societies around the world is critical for nurturing our creative potential from our earliest days until our final ones.

Pursuits that allow us to be creative light a spark within. When such a spark becomes a flame, we take our dreams into the world and companies, governments, communities, and societies are forever changed.

Service to Others

Engaging in community service or volunteering our time—in homeless shelters, soup kitchens, hospitals, schools, and homes for the elderly—we experience the power of extending positive focused energy to another human being in need.

While it is impossible for any act of service to be wholly selfless, since the giver is inevitably enriched, when we give without seeking anything in return, we experience the feelings that naturally emerge from the 3D mind: compassion, empathy, love, kindness, and a sense that we are all the same at the most fundamental human level. In this way, service activities not only make the world a better place, they also enrich our inner world by taking us into the 3D mind and harnessing our positive focused energy.

Exercise

The power of physical exercise has been reaffirmed time and again. Countless research studies show that its positive benefits extend far beyond the body. It makes us feel better and relaxes the mind. Not only is exercise a powerful antidote to most chronic diseases, including many cancers, it also improves our cognitive abilities, lifts our mood, and reduces depression, anxiety, and insomnia.

Exercises that lead us into the 3D mind are ones that don't need our continuous attention, such as hiking, walking, running, biking, and swimming. Team sports are good for our health but, since we have to pay continuous attention during a game, they tend to allow for fewer moments of stillness. Even for an activity such as running, doing so on a safe, relaxing trail can take us into the 3D mind; running through a crowded city requires our constant attention and keeps us in the 1D or 2D mind.

Mind-Body Practices

Many mind-body practices, such as yoga, qigong, and tai chi, are powerful paths out of the 1D and 2D minds. In parallel they also lead us into the 3D mind because such practices encourage us to focus on stilling the mind. Since it is the one I know best, I will share a few thoughts on yoga here.

Yoga's origins date back thousands of years to ancient India. In its true Sanskrit origins, the word *yog* means union with our inner energy. Ancient writings on yoga's physical postures emphasize that their purpose is to eliminate the fluctuations of the mind and to promote inner stillness. I practiced yoga's physical postures for many years but came to appreciate its true powers only when I learned to teach it.

Yoga's stretching and balancing postures strengthen and relax many different muscles and tissues in the body. In addition, its focus on deep breathing helps reduce stress and bring our attention inward. Our muscles gain flexibility and endurance. Deep breathing calms our nerves and improves our immune and endocrine systems. In recent years, many clinical trials have been conducted around the world to study the beneficial effects of yoga and they are revealing its powerful role in helping to heal many physical and mental ailments including chronic pain, insomnia, irritable bowel syndrome, depression, and anxiety.

Yoga's physical postures are not designed to aspire to or attain any specific levels of flexibility. It has no metrics of progress, because the postures are just the journey. The destination is the 3D mind. In fact, one of the most powerful yoga postures is the last one—when we lie down flat on our backs and remain motionless. The body relaxed by exercise, the breath eased by relaxation, and the mind calmed by both lead us toward stillness. The 1D and 2D minds subside. The 3D mind emerges. We can feel this benefit after just one session.

Guiding us to observe how our physical state affects our mental state (and vice versa) is yoga's most profound teaching. Yoga teaches us to breathe and balance through challenges, physically on the mat and figuratively in life. Balancing postures are easier when we feel calm; flexibility increases when we release our grip on both muscles and thoughts; breathing becomes relaxed when we give our mind a break. In this way, yoga is one of the most powerful paths into the 3D mind.

Yet while all these pursuits engage both our body and mind, there is another way—one that allows us to access the 3D mind most directly—the path of stillness, which we explore next.

Chapter Twelve

Into the Mind

Everything has its wonders, even darkness and silence, and
I learn, whatever state I may be in, therein to be content.
—Helen Keller

We move through much of our lives without taking a pause—when the mind becomes still, tranquility enters, and silence prevails. One of the most powerful paths for quieting the 1D and 2D minds and entering the 3D mind is to bring serenity into the mind and direct positive focused energy at it—the path of stillness. Stillness is a state of physical motionlessness accompanied by mental alertness (i.e., sleeping doesn't count).

Practices of stillness are as old as humanity and exist in countless variants. Stillness has fueled artists, poets, writers, and inventors through the centuries. Most of the world's spiritual traditions teach it. We can call it prayer, meditation, contemplation, or mindfulness. Different faiths or schools of thought might guide us to a unique focus point or teach it with their own guidelines, rituals, and rules.

Yet they all lead us to the same place. Stillness calms our body and releases the 1D mind's survival instincts and their associated stress responses. When we first practice stillness, the 2D mind's thought factory may go into overdrive. But we soon learn how to shut it down. Then nothing but silence remains and the stage is set for the 3D mind to enter. In the beginning, the experience of being in the 3D mind might appear as a fleeting flicker, but as we practice we learn to access it more proactively.

For reasons fundamental to stillness, the simpler we keep our journey, the lower our chances of getting distracted, lost, or disenchanted. Stillness is designed to still the activities of our senses and is most powerful when practiced in solitude. Many people say that it is hard to find the time every day to sit still with their eyes closed. Or they say that they have tried it a few times but it "didn't work," felt pointless, or was too frustrating. Still others worry that they are doing it "wrong." All of this, and none of this, makes sense. In an "on the go" world where "fast food" is not an oxymoron, activity is mistaken for productivity, and being busy is often a badge of importance, it can be hard to comprehend how doing nothing can do anything for us. At least we can see and assess physical activity. How do we measure the output of solitary silence?

This is how the 2D mind thinks. Furthermore, sometimes we fear stillness. It might be subtle fear and anxiety around inner unknowns, unprocessed emotions, undigested pain, and what they might do to us if we examined them. This is the 1D mind begging for your attention. But here's the truth: silence is the eternal soundtrack of the universe. We all began our lives in it—suspended in our mother's womb until we entered the world with a scream. We all end in it. Beyond the cacophony of daily life on Earth, most of the universe is stillness, and even nature's vast factories—trees, flowers, and plants—conduct their work in near quietude.

Silence is a natural state, more natural than so many others we pick up during years of living. When we forget it in our lives, we deprive ourselves. To attain it, we don't have to go chase anything. We just have to remove distractions, let our guard down, cast our fears aside, and quiet our ego. Then stillness fills the void—it dawns on us. To discover it, wherever and however we are, we just need to begin.

Steps to Stillness

Here, the concepts on stillness are distilled to their most basic essence: five simple steps to go within. Many more detailed discussions are readily available elsewhere. When just beginning to learn stillness, you may also want to have a teacher or guide show you the way.

1. Still the Body

Stillness begins by finding a comfortable position in which our body can become completely motionless. Try to find a peaceful space where you will be undisturbed for as long as you would like to practice stillness. It could be 10, 20, or 30 minutes at home or just a few minutes in a parked car. (Note: Please don't attempt stillness while you are in any situation that requires your alert attention, such as driving, operating machinery, crossing a street—you get the idea.) It is best to lie flat on the floor or to sit in a comfortable position, either on the floor or in a chair, as long as you keep your back and spine straight. If lying down will make you fall asleep, then sit.

Once settled, try to let go of and relax all your muscles. Observe where the attention of your senses (sight, sound, smell, taste, and touch) is directed. Then try to disengage from each one of them. Avoid having any distracting scents or sounds in your space and close your eyes. Also, don't hold on to anything, so your hands can relax too. Imagine any physical tension dissolving like ice melting into water. Relax. Let go. Smile gently. And take long, deep breaths.

2. Focus on Breathing

In the course of our lives, we will do more breathing than any other activity over which we exert some direct control. Why not make the most of it? Deep and rhythmic breathing helps to calm our body and exerts a powerful physiological relaxation response (the opposite of the stress response). It reduces stress, promotes inner balance and takes us out of the 1D and 2D minds.

To deepen and relax our breathing, it is best to focus on deep abdominal breaths. Most of us tend to breathe in and out of the upper part of our torso—the chest and lung area. In abdominal breathing, we can see and feel our abdomen extending outward as the lower part of our torso fills with air. Compared with shallower chest breathing, abdominal breathing engages the full capacity of our lungs. Babies are expert abdominal breathers, and we can see their tummies rise and fall as they breathe. Changing how we breathe takes no extra effort or time. We all have time to breathe better, because we are already breathing anyway. Thus, we can start right here, right now—with our next breath, and the next one.

To deepen your breathing, inhale slowly to the count of five, hold your breath for a count, and then exhale to the count of ten. This brings a steady rhythm to breath. Many different counts and ratios for inhaling, holding, and exhaling exist. Their shared purpose is to bring regularity, relaxation, and depth to breath.

We can practice breathing better while sitting in a meeting or at our desk, commuting, driving, waiting in line, lying in bed, reading a book, or anytime we remember. And, of course, while practicing stillness.

3. Watch Your Thoughts

Just as nonstop work wears down the body, constant thinking exhausts the mind. As your body settles into stillness, become an observer of your mind. This begins to slow down your thoughts. It is as if they become aware that you are watching them.

Don't judge or analyze your thoughts. Just observe them passing by. Imagine your mind as a blank movie screen across which your thoughts are playing like movies; whether they are comedies, romances, tragedies, or action-filled thrillers, each is a glimpse of an experience that comes and goes.

When we first practice stillness, our mind finds the idea of quieting itself profoundly counterintuitive. The 2D mind initiates all sorts of conversations to remind us that it exists: *Hey, don't you need me right now? On the one hand, you can ignore me, but on the other hand, why would you? I am you.*

If I don't think, who are you? Analyze this. Don't let me go just like that.

The mind does not stop there. You might recall forgotten errands, neglected relatives, and even mundane tasks and thoughts with renewed urgency. The 1D mind chimes in with forgotten fears and needs. Aches and pains may emerge. Irresistible itches appear. Any concern that the mind can generate will likely pay you a visit. But these are fleeting visitors. Just observe them and remain aware. Thoughts come and go. Just remember: You are not your thoughts—you are their observer. You are not your mind—you are its guide.

4. Pause Your Thoughts

As we calm the 1D and 2D minds, we attain some distance from them. Once we pause our usual mental programming, we can access positive focused energy to reach the 3D mind:

1. *Positive*: When a negative thought enters the mind, think of its positive antidote. Negative thoughts tend to arrive in armies. Positive thoughts are often happy alone. One positive thought can eradicate a brigade of negative ones.

2. *Focused:* When the mind is wandering, bring your attention to a focus point, such as paying attention to your breath; repeating a positive word or affirmation (e.g., "I am relaxed"); or listening to soft music (ideally, without distracting lyrics). Sometimes it even helps to focus on an imaginary inner point. Each time your mind wanders, gently bring it back to this point.

3. *Energy:* As we become more peaceful and relaxed, we feel a shift in our inner energy. Anxiety and restlessness subside. Serenity, joy, and peacefulness enter. We gain greater awareness of our surroundings and our selves. Our perspective expands. In this way, stillness rejuvenates and energizes us. It increases our inner energy and harnesses positive focused energy.

5. Practice

As with any skill, the power of stillness grows with practice. But we can "practice" even in the smallest windows of time. How do we fill the still moments in our life? We all have them: commuting to work, waiting in line, lying in bed, sitting in the bathroom, taking a shower—times when we can get away with not actively thinking about the task at hand. We tend to fill them with texting, e-mail, talking, music, reading, and myriad other activities.

Yet how we spend the pauses of our days reflects how we live our lives. When those pauses are still, we live in peace. When we constantly fill them with noise and distractions, we lose ourselves.

If we cannot find the time to set aside for practicing stillness, we can at least fill the brief pauses that already exist in our days with it. We can close our eyes for a moment. Breathe deeply. Smile. Even stilling our thoughts for a few minutes can revitalize us.

The more we practice stillness, the more we discover its powers. Over time, the 1D mind loosens its control, the 2D mind becomes less bossy, and the 3D mind begins to reveal its wisdom and insights.

What We Ingest

It is impossible to talk about enhancing the powers of our mind without considering what we put into our body. This is because what we feed our body influences our state of mind and certain dietary practices seem to promote mental calmness. Food is the medicine we take every day, three or more times a day.

It is also impossible to do justice to this vast field in a few pages. Thus a few principles—ones that most consistently emerged from my research—are mentioned here so you can explore them further. Some may work for you, others may not. These are not the only principles that matter; they are just ones I discovered during this journey. To determine what influences your mind, and how, let your experience be your guide. The knowledge of what is good for us is within each of us. We are each an expert on our self. We just have to learn to trust our expertise. With increased awareness, when we pause and listen, answers emerge.

Instead of viewing food through the drives and urges of the 1D mind, which leads us to eat for pleasure, out of boredom, or to cope with stress, we can consider it with the wisdom of the 3D mind, which sees food as a source of nourishment for physical and mental well-being. When our body is nourished with nutritious foods, our mind can attain greater alertness and clarity. Eating more whole, natural foods, such as fresh fruits and vegetables, promotes mental health.

The evidence-based talks from the lifestyle medicine conference of the prior chapter suggest a trend toward vegetarian diets composed of vegetables, beans, and whole grains. Significant meat consumption may adversely affect mental functioning. Excess sugar, caffeine, and alcohol also interfere with the mind's serenity. Many highly processed, high-calorie, low-nutrient foods can leave our body feeling tired and our mind lethargic.

Eating a healthy, nutritious breakfast provides energy to start the day. The biggest meal of the day is usually best consumed as lunch. A lighter dinner taken early in the evening promotes restful sleep. Going to bed with a full, heavy stomach can disturb sleep and lead to restless dreams.

Water is one of the best beverages for adults. Drinking six to eight glasses per day (or enough so your urine's almost clear, as a doctor friend once told me) is ideal. Proper hydration helps improve mental clarity. Dehydration can promote a vast spectrum of mental ailments, including irritability, migraines, and even depression.

When we are eating, it helps to direct our attention to the food we are about to consume. Fully chewing each bite slows our eating pace, aids digestion, and enhances our sense of nourishment. Eating while multitasking, working, or looking at a screen can create stress within or lead to mindless eating. With increased awareness, when reaching for food, we recognize why we are eating.

While metabolism and nutritional needs vary among individuals, eating excessive calories is often a result of mis-alignment in one or more of the above areas. When we burn the calories we consume, we tend to maintain our weight. As we focus on the state of our mind, we tend to become more aware of how the foods we consume influence our mental functioning. With increased awareness of what we eat—and why—we learn which foods make us feel good or bad.

Feeding the Mind

We pay careful attention to many visible and tangible details in our lives, yet often we neglect to carefully watch what we put into our mind. As much as what we eat, what we feed our mind through our senses also affects us.

I once heard a story about a father telling his son about two wolves who live in our mind, jostling and wrestling for control over us. One of them represents good, and the other represents evil. "Which one wins?" the child asks. "The one you feed," the father responds. It is the same with the states of our mind. When we generate positive focused energy, we are energized and positivity emanates. If we feed the needs of the 1D mind, we can become adversely influenced by negativity, aggression, or violence, which weaken our mind.

Watching excessive violence on TV or in movies, or playing violent video games, affects our mental state. We may not realize it, but just as positive inputs energize us, negative inputs may provide a short-term adrenaline boost but eventually drain us and often drag us lower. Just as awareness changes what we feed our bodies, it can help shift what we feed our mind, so that we seek more experiences that elicit joy, contentment, and serenity.

Resting the Mind

The final mind-related activity that needs mention is sleep. Getting seven to eight hours of sleep each night gives the mind a chance to refresh and reboot. While pulling an all-nighter in my first job out of college, I remember seeing a graph posted in a colleague's cubicle that showed how sleep deprivation caused the same mental degradation and loss of hand-eye coordination as being drunk. A tired mind is essentially a drunk mind. In the long run, we don't gain time by sleeping less. We lose time because the quality of our waking hours declines and we need more time to do less work. To attain peak performance, we need to be well rested and alert.

Sleep holds another powerful secret. The zone between being awake and being asleep—when we are both falling into sleep and coming out of it—encourages stillness and can lead us into the 3D mind. Since the 1D and 2D minds are often quiet in that zone, the 3D mind can emerge. This is why we often get ideas while waking up and many great minds have talked about such experiences.

For instance, in his autobiography, Mahatma Gandhi wrote that one of his earliest civil disobedience ideas came to him in this state: "That night I fell asleep while thinking over the question. Towards the small hours of the morning I woke up somewhat earlier than usual. I was still in that twilight condition between sleep and consciousness when suddenly the idea broke upon me—it was as if in a dream."[33] By becoming more aware of our state of mind and by focusing on stilling it both when we fall asleep and as we awake, we can each tap into the creative power of this zone.

Who we are in this world is inevitably a reflection of what goes on in our mind. The most powerful minds of the future will be ones that know how to nurture and nourish, train and sustain themselves to harness their highest potential. They will create the paths of progress for humanity. How we can each create such paths is next.

V. Arrival

CHAPTER THIRTEEN

Creating Paths

We are all inventors, each sailing out on a voyage of discovery,
guided each by a private chart, of which there is no duplicate.
—Ralph Waldo Emerson

On July 4, 1845, in what would become one of the most famous retreats in American history, a scruffy 28-year-old moved into a small wooden hut to "transact some private business with the fewest obstacles."[34] His mission: an "experiment" to live as simply as possible, to "drive life into a corner, and reduce it to its lowest terms."[35] Two years later, for his 10th college reunion report, summarizing the years since graduation, he wrote:

> I don't know whether mine is a profession, or a trade, or what not.... I am a Schoolmaster–a Private Tutor, a Surveyor–a Gardener, a Farmer–a Painter, I mean a House Painter, a Carpenter, a Mason, a Day-Laborer, a Pencil-Maker, a Glass-paper Maker, a Writer, and sometimes a Poetaster.... Indeed my

steadiest employment, if such it can be called, is to keep myself at the top of my condition, and ready for whatever may turn up in heaven or on earth. For the last two or three years I have lived in Concord woods, alone, something more than a mile from any neighbor, in a house built entirely by myself.... P. S. I beg that the Class will not consider me an object of charity, and if any of them are in want of pecuniary assistance, and will make known their case to me, I will engage to give them some advice of more worth than money.[36]

This jack-of-all-trades who renounced the "beaten track" and listened to a "different drummer"—to use his own words—became, in the annals of history, the most famous graduate of the Harvard University class of 1837. His account of those two years in the woods, *Walden*, is filled with deep philosophical wisdom and extraordinary insights on the "wildness" whose "tonic" he drank. Today, it is a timeless classic and ranks among America's most famous literary works.

In his many writings over the years, Henry David Thoreau conveyed simple yet profound observations on humanity—ones that traveled across time and space—inspiring Mahatma Gandhi's civil disobedience movement to free India from British rule, which in turn influenced Martin Luther King Jr. and the civil rights movement in the United States, in essence creating ripples that might be said to have altered the very course of human history.

How do we each find and create our own true paths in life? By embarking on this journey, I realized that we learn less from the details of others' lives and more from the patterns they reveal. To find our path, the best wisdom we can gain from the stories of others is not how we can walk in their footsteps but how they learned to walk their own paths.

Thoreau, Gandhi, and Dr. King all embodied values that drew on the strengths of their 1D, 2D, and 3D minds. Perhaps this is why the words of each resonated so deeply with the one who followed him. Each held steadfast belief in his ideas and ideals. They were courageous men who had tamed their 1D minds. All landed in jail, the latter two several times. Gandhi and Dr. King's words suggest they had conquered fear; both were ready to die for their cause—and did. Thoreau and Gandhi lived exceedingly simple lives to meet their barest needs. Dr. King donated the money from his Nobel Peace Prize to his movement and left none behind upon his death.

Their rich yet simple inner lives gave each immense focus. All three devoted significant time to knowing themselves. Gandhi saw it as a prerequisite to leading any change in the world. Dr. King's career itself was a spiritual path. Both Gandhi and Dr. King became the faces of causes much greater than their identities. They saw themselves as the means to realizing a greater dream. Thoreau's immersion in nature imbued him with deep perspective. All three had trained the weaknesses of their 2D minds.

Lastly, and most powerfully, reading each of their words leaves no doubt that their wisdom emerged from their deepest truths, convictions, and beliefs. Each saw a path to a better future that tapped into the fundamental goodness of humanity. Each realized the potential it held for transforming society. And each looked for ways to bring it into the world. Thoreau, Gandhi, and Dr. King had not only learned to trust their 3D minds, each was an embodiment of its immense power. Gandhi and Dr. King tirelessly spoke of the power of love to lift humanity. Both saw their mission as even greater than the freedom and equality movements they helped to lead. Their deep love of humanity emerged from a fundamental belief that each human soul deserves equal compassion, respect, and dignity.

The battles we are fighting in the world today are different from those of eras past. Or so we might say if we consider that India is independent and the United States has made strides in social justice. But the truth is, our timeless battles remain the same. They are of the better nature of humanity against our darker side; they encompass the pursuit of our basic needs and then of the higher ones that lend meaning to life and encourage the uplifting of humanity.

The fundamental causes echoed in Thoreau, Gandhi and Dr. King's words remain the greatest challenges of our times as well: ensuring justice, equality, freedom, and individual dignity for each and every one of us. Thus we each owe it to ourselves, and, more important, to our fellow human beings, to ask ourselves what we can do to advance the progress of humanity—to live a life of true meaning and purpose.

Why?

Why is it so difficult for the rest of us to even explore the paths that Thoreau, Gandhi, and Dr. King so boldly walked? Our established thought patterns and tendencies, and the expectations and measuring sticks of society, can become like ancient rivers flowing through our minds. The longer they flow along a certain path or way of thinking, the more deeply they carve their way. Crevices turn into gorges over time. Trodden paths appear easier to follow, especially with the 1D or 2D mind. It is usually easier to keep a job than to quit it to pursue a dream. Fear sets in and the ego worries about our reputation. *What will others think or say?* We often go through life painting meticulously within the lines of our coloring books without pausing often enough to consider whether we want to redraw the lines themselves. Ever-rising yardsticks of our "basic needs," self-interest, and fear of what might go wrong keep us "in line."

Thoreau, Gandhi, and Dr. King often said that they knew—in the depths of their being—they were on their life's mission. They had unshakable conviction and faith. Naysayers, critics, and doubters could not deter them.

The journey of finding your life's mission is one you have embarked on by virtue of having arrived at the words you are reading here, now. Your next step—identifying your true mission—is as simple as asking yourself a singular question: *Why do I do what I do?* The answers are there already. You just need to go find them.

The process of truly probing this question begins by relinquishing fear and setting aside the ego. To discover meaningful answers, we have to commit ourselves to the question. The first time we ponder it, we might get preliminary answers. But for each answer we obtain, we need to ask again: Why? Children are experts at asking simple, innocent questions that distill the complexity of the world. "Why does that girl not have shoes?" or "Why are you angry?" As adults we often become enmeshed in the what, when, where, and how. We forget to ask why.

We will each get through life on some path, yet we owe it to ourselves—and to the world—to seriously ask and answer why we do what we do in our lives. While this question applies to anything we pursue in life, let us explore it here in the context of careers, of finding our life's mission in our work. Let us consider it in three parts:

Why Do...

Why does it matter to you? Do you work for survival, for a paycheck (1D), for external validation, to attain a particular metric of success (2D), or because your work resonates in the depths of your being and feels like your life's mission (3D)? When we seek more in life—whether money, power, prestige, status, recognition, or fame—how often, before entering the race for it, do we stop and ask: Why? Truly, why? Are our "whys" driven by external factors, or do they emerge from within? When we fail to realize the dreams in our hearts, we go through the motions of life without being fully alive. And we are each craving to act out of our deepest, truest convictions, rather than to satisfy external standards and expectations that fail to resonate within.

I Do...

Does the work you do feel like a job (1D), a career (2D), or your calling (3D)? When our work engages our talents, skills, and creative abilities, we unleash our highest potential and find meaning, purpose, and personal fulfillment in it. When our work is our calling, we are filled with passion, it feels effortless, and it becomes play. It gives us courage to create new paths and resilience to strive through failure. If we sense internal misalignment, then we can ask: Why? When our work is aligned with who we are, we are fueled by positive focused energy.

What I Do?

Why does your work matter to the world? Does it advance the greater good of humanity? As you contemplate this, seek brutally honest responses to this question. The 2D mind tends to rationalize, and sometimes we can fool ourselves into logical answers that don't echo our truths. This can lead us—as individuals and even as organizations—to engage in work that strays from our true mission. Fulfillment in our work comes when we know and believe that it makes a meaningful difference in the lives of others.

Finding our passion is truly as simple as answering this single question. Rather than halfheartedly pondering it for a lifetime, when we pause and ask ourselves with positive focused energy, the 3D mind guides us to answers. In the 1D mind, it is impossible to derive meaningful answers, because this question goes beyond survival. The 2D mind can be more productive, but it usually keeps us in a confined zone of the known and familiar, where our ego feels safe. It can drive us toward work that looks prestigious and impressive but does not feel fulfilling or meaningful.

When we probe our answers more deeply layers peel away and our truths emerge. Once we find our real, honest answers, our work and life align around our mission. Our reasons for doing and being become one: we do what we do because of who we are, and we are who we are because of what we do. We cannot imagine doing anything else. We allow the 3D mind to guide us and discover new paths for our journeys.

When we live primarily in the 1D and 2D minds, we look to the outside world for answers. We look for role models, mentors, gurus, or guides who can give us directions toward what we seek or out of what we want to escape. That is the equivalent of seeking a pill. The wisdom we can learn from them, from history, and even from philosophy and religion is not where to go but how to find our path to our wisdom. Once clarity appears within, we see obstacles as opportunities, failures as teachers, and darkness as light. In the 3D mind, fear, doubt, and the ego turn from massive boulders that can block our path to pebbles that merely brush against our shoes.

There is one guarantee about this journey: you will have one steadfast friend along the way. This friend's name is Failure, and it will be your greatest teacher.

Our Friend Failure

Thoreau was a prolific writer. He kept a regular journal and published articles for many different magazines and journals. During his days at Walden Pond, he worked on the manuscript for his first book, *A Week on the Concord and Merrimack Rivers*. After several rejections, that book was published in 1849, about two years after he had returned from Walden. "One thousand copies were printed at the author's risk. Of these, seventy-five were given away, two hundred and nineteen were sold, and the remaining seven hundred and six were returned to Thoreau on October 28, 1853."[37] When Thoreau received the books, he was still in debt to his publisher. That day, he wrote in his journal, "They are something more substantial than fame, as my back knows, which has borne them up two flights of stairs to a place quite similar to that to which they trace their origin.... I have now a library of nearly nine hundred volumes, over seven hundred of which I wrote myself."[38]

The life we plan is often different from what unfolds through the chapters of our days. Many might have put the pen to rest in the face of such failure. Yet Thoreau continued, "in spite of this result, sitting beside the inert mass of my works, I take up my pen to-night to record what thought or experience I have had with as much satisfaction as ever. Indeed, I believe that the result is more inspiring and better for me than if a thousand had bought my wares. It affects my privacy less and leaves me freer."[39]

Walden was published the following year, and the rest, as they say, is history. The poor reception of his first book was a pebble Thoreau kicked to the side of his path. For him, the journey was the destination.

We spend much of our time planning for destinations, yet for most of what matters in life, it is in the journeys themselves that we discover meaning. Our most profound experiences often cannot be planned. In any journey, if things are always going as planned and we face no obstacles along the way, one of two truths likely emerges—we are walking along a safe, well-trodden path or we are not going anywhere.

On any path that holds the potential for transformation, derailment and stumbling are inevitable. Once we gain the courage to explore varied routes to our eventual destinations, we realize that detours and rough terrain hold lessons in themselves. Sometimes it is only in getting knocked down that we eventually find our true destinations. Thus, it helps to befriend failure and to understand its traits so we can keep charging ahead when the going gets tough.

During my venture capital days, I would typically explore hundreds of inventions before investing in a few. Even among the chosen ones, statistically, more fail than succeed. Products implode during development, management teams fall apart, and marketing strategies flop. Many startups attain their ultimate success with strategies or products that bear only a faint resemblance to their original business plans. As soon as we decide to try something new, we are, by definition, treading into the terrain of failure. This is the law of being a change agent. The world of startups is a classroom filled with failure, and by virtue of investing in them, one becomes an expert at it. The lessons gathered from such failures hold universal wisdom.

One of the most powerful lessons I learned is that the difference between failure and success is what we do when we fail. Failure becomes failure only when we burden it with the weight of finality. When we think of failure and success as two sides of the same coin, we can focus on doing our best and leave the rest to chance. Irrespective of how the coin falls during a given toss, we keep going, knowing that it could also fall the other way. Even if we hit a string of failures, we remember that if we stay in the game, success will eventually show up.

This spirit is embodied by athletes, such as Olympic figure skaters. Each skater enters the competition with a carefully choreographed sequence practiced countless times in advance. But when it comes to the final performance on the Olympic ice, even the best stumble and fall. Yet the music keeps playing. Fallen athletes swiftly get up—physically and, more important, mentally—regain their smile, resynchronize their body with the beat, and dance until the music ends.

Why, then, in our often-less-shaky lives, where the getting up often needs to take place only inside and not before an audience of millions, do we hesitate to jump up and keep going? Why do we often become overwhelmed by failures large and small? The difference between staying down and getting up is in our mind. It is our level of positive focused energy. In essence, it reflects our ability to move from the 1D and 2D minds into the 3D mind.

The 1D and 2D minds dislike failure. The 1D mind resists change and avoids any actions that create the potential for failure. The 2D mind may worry about reputation, what others will think and say, and the price to be paid. The 3D mind embraces failure, because it recognizes it as a vital force for transformation. Thoreau viewed not having sold all the copies of his first book as such a gift. Stories of people who have overcome incredible odds inspire us. Thoreau's experience with failure is not the exception among history's greats—it is the norm. Success does not appear despite life's failures—it arises from them.

Many entrepreneurs, leaders, and role models, when asked about their success, trace it back to such moments—their darkest hours, when they were knocked down and then built a dream, vision, and path for not just rising but reaching higher. Success comes by considering failure a teacher, mentor, and best friend—a companion on all our journeys. The 1D and 2D minds create and attach labels of failure or success to our lives. The 3D mind sees any event as merely an experience. If an experience teaches us something, the 3D mind deems it a success. It becomes a failure only if we fail to learn its lessons. In fact, once we have completed formal schooling, failures are among life's best teachers. In the varied curriculum of life, if we ignore a lesson it may keep coming back to instill the same teaching in different ways. Sometimes we take the same exam over and over again, until we absorb its lessons. The sooner we learn from our mistakes, the faster we pass such exams and move on. Eat the cookie and get back on the diet. Get angry and return to peace. As we learn from each mistake, we really learn how to succeed.

The hidden blessing of failure is that it puts us in the high-speed lane for self-improvement. Failure makes one reflect, contemplate, and introspect in a way that victory rarely does. Success often breeds arrogance and complacency. When life is going well, when success comes easily, we often don't bother to stop and ask questions.

Failure brings humility and improvement. Those in suffering, crisis, or pain, while trying to grapple with challenges, are led to ask life's profound questions and to ponder them deeply. When what we know is not enough, we try to know more, to understand differently, and to become open to new possibilities. We look for ways to discover or create new paths in our lives.

Most human failures fall into a few basic categories: we fail in our work, at relationships, or in meeting our goals. Sometimes disruptions such as illness diagnoses, accidents, or circumstances beyond our direct control derail our life plans. At other times, our "failure" is simply the feeling that we are stuck in a rut or on a stagnant path, unable to change. The fear of a worse outcome can keep us in a mediocre status quo—a job, a relationship, a life—that nags at us but is not bad enough to propel change. Sometimes it takes a crisis to shove us out. We are forced to step back and reflect, to explore new horizons, and to see the same old challenges from new perspectives. Then where we once saw stagnation, we discover potential and, over time, outlines of new paths.

Yet why are the most powerful lessons we learn in life often such painful ones? It is because during moments of pain or crisis we can gain immense clarity. A vivid experience is powerfully etched into us. Lasting transformation then takes root in the 3D mind. Obstacles become potential detours, not permanent roadblocks. This distinction spells the difference between staying down and rising when we fall.

Failure is one of our greatest fears. Once we realize how precious and powerful failure can be, we discover there is nothing to fear. Religions, philosophies, entrepreneurship guides, and innovation manuals, at their essence, hold the same message: To access our potential, we have to be positive and unlock and open our minds. We have to trust the answers we obtain and be focused—to channel our potential to transform it into reality.

With these simple ideas, we can each begin our journey toward true success. Like Thoreau, Gandhi, and Dr. King, we feel fearless and free, are filled with inspiration and courage, and can create new thoughts and paths in our minds and in the world—ones we truly wish to walk.

CHAPTER FOURTEEN

We Wish to Walk

This above all: to thine own self be true, And it must follow, as the night the day, Thou canst not then be false to any man.
—William Shakespeare

The matter of finding and creating our own paths gains earnest momentum when we take our first steps into the "real world" and bring the ideals of youth into the industries, institutions, and systems that build and uphold society. We witness, for the first time, the gap between our idealization of how the world works and its reality. I first experienced this when I entered Wall Street for a year right out of college, and then observed it repeatedly over the years through my own experiences and those of peers scaling the most coveted strata of society.

In the beginning, there is often puzzlement (*Is this how it works?*), followed by shock (*Is this* really *how it works?!?*). Over time we compromise (*I guess this is how it works*) and often accept and even endorse (*This is how it* must *work*). At first, a reluctance to participate in "how it works," especially when "it" goes against our inner voice or what we believe, can be tormenting. The higher one moves in a profession's hierarchy, the more is revealed and the more is at stake. When our inner and outer worlds clash, some walk out. Others continue walking along, knowing they are treading carefully construed, ever-shifting, and frequently rationalized moral boundaries: *I'll do this just once. Everyone else is doing it too. This is the only way to survive—I don't have a choice.* Yet the repercussions of our actions reshape the very trajectory of our lives and the world.

The point here is not about how Wall Street's greed erodes trust in financial institutions, how corporations foster mistrust by promoting opacity, or how a revolving door for talent and capital between the private and public sectors corrodes confidence in both. The question is: why do essentially good people end up engaging in dubious or bad actions with unforeseen or even disastrous consequences? How do we land in jobs that provide money without meaning or power without purpose?

What leads a stock trader to pursue legal yet unethical practices, a scientist to cherry-pick data, a doctor to perform unnecessary procedures, an executive to do one thing yet believe another, and a politician to promise and not deliver? At the same time, what leads some people to walk away from the same "carrots" or "sticks" that handcuff others? What gives some the courage to speak up or raise uncomfortable truths where no one else has dared before, thus risking their careers for the greater good?

The humans behind the structures and systems of our society share the same timeless aspirations. We all hunger for a deeper sense of meaning in life—a connection to our truest self, our inner being. Many of us spend a lifetime trying to satisfy the needs of the 1D and 2D minds, only to discover that the true "hunger" within us was that of connecting to the 3D mind.

When we are driven by the 1D mind, untamed fear can lead to timidity and untamed hunger to greed. When we are driven by the 2D mind, our thought factory concerns itself with prestige, reputation, and peer approval. Yet when untrained, it can lead us to feed our ego more than serves us, make us prey to greed, or rationalize whatever we do, including transgressions of our moral boundaries. Then we shift from seeking truths to looking for information that supports and rationalizes our actions. Yet this comes at the expense of the very essence of who we are. Stress is often a symptom of such inner discord.

When we listen to and pursue the mission emerging from our 3D mind, we attain peace and contentment. We gain the courage to stand for our beliefs and to speak our truths. As we direct more attention to the 3D mind, it becomes easier to trust it and to tame and train the 1D and 2D minds. Then we can tap into our true inner power.

One day in the spring of 2014, while teaching a class on authentic leadership, I remembered the advice I had received from the wise physicist we met in the opening pages. He had said that to attain our dreams, we must visualize them so intensely that we experience them in the depths of our being. I realized that our ability to do so emerges from the same source that empowers us to speak our truths in the world and to be led by our 3D mind. That source, which also imbues us with the confidence and courage to walk our paths, is authenticity.

How Can We Be Authentic?

Humanity has always celebrated authentic voices—people who find and follow the song in their hearts. Authenticity does not come to us from the outside in; it emerges from within. Authenticity is an expression of our integrity. It is aligning who we think we are with who we say we are and what we actually do. It defines what we stand for, what we believe in, and why. At its best, authenticity reveals the power of what is possible when our highest potential is unlocked and unleashed, within us and in those around us. It is the deepest expression of our most human essence.

We often seek to be truly understood by others. Yet if we don't even know who we are, how can anyone else understand us? Sometimes, we look to others or the outside world to help us be our best selves. Yet if we are not the first to do that for ourselves, we become perpetually dependent on the ever-changing outside world to define us. When we face another person, a job, an idea, an organization, or a system without really knowing ourselves, we absorb the light of the world. When we know our selves, we shine our light onto it.

As we are deluged with more data than ever in our 21st century lives, and as our minds are continuously stimulated, it has become easier than ever to just observe the chatter of others' minds—their thoughts, status updates, tweets, and emotional reactions. Yet while it may be harder, it is more important than ever to find and speak our own authentic voice. In an ocean of so many voices, how do we find our own, rather than echoing others' or the latest thought trends? And once we find it, how do we develop the courage to speak it?

It has been said many times in many ways that the easiest and hardest work on Earth is to travel within—to truly know ourselves. We discover our authentic self when we have the courage to face ourselves—all of ourselves—the good and the bad. Beyond knowing our likes and dislikes, or even our goals and ambitions, facing ourselves is a process of delving into what we stand for, and why. It is an honest and open-minded exploration into what defines us at our most fundamental level.

We can begin this journey by bringing awareness to our thoughts and words. Often we just speak words generated by our 1D and 2D minds, which are easily swayed. Sometimes such words don't even accurately reflect what we truly believe. Or, when we face conflicts involving others, we look for blame, answers, and explanations in the "other" side. Yet only when our finger points back at us can we focus on better understanding ourselves and how to live our values in the world.

Undertaking such inner exploration also extends to organizations and societies. In our approaches to solving challenges, we often look for 3D mind ideas with 2D mind processes and 1D mind filters. Sometimes fear drives the herd mentality. Fear of missing out lets good money follow bad, or fear of risking a reputation leads to advocating unoriginal ideas that perpetuate the status quo. Or we rely on approval by others. To avoid appearing crazy, rather than sharing original thoughts, we repeat those of others. Such mental conformity is often referred to as groupthink—the tendency of a group's members to validate each other's thoughts and ideas. Yet when we avoid disagreement and disapproval, we lose the potential of so many minds. From

Silicon Valley to Wall Street, groupthink can have disastrous consequences, especially when the group consists of intelligent, successful people, many of whom are considered experts.

Companies and organizations often hire employees because they seem moldable. Malleability falls into two camps. One consists of individuals who are open to learning from others' minds, which is critical to success. The other consists of people who fail to stand by the strength of their convictions, simply agree with their peers, or keep quiet despite their intuitions. Such behaviors lead to a lack of diversity of thought, which seems even more pervasive than a lack of other kinds of diversity in America's workforce and perpetuates the equivalent of old boys' clubs: Old Brains Clubs.

How Do We Lead the Way?

The authentic voice from within is fearless. When led by our 3D mind, we do things for the right reasons and out of wisdom. Our mental immune system becomes stronger, and others influence us less. When we release our fears and think independently, we can change the world, as history reminds us. We become catalysts. In chemical reactions, a catalyst can transform other molecules without being changed, and it can repeat this process many times. It is the same with human catalysts. When we become one, we can inspire change in others and help them transform into catalysts themselves. Together, we begin to lift humanity.

Gandhi is one of recent history's greatest exemplars of the power of this principle and he described it eloquently in his autobiography: "All the tendencies present in the outer world are to be found in the world of our body. If we could change ourselves, the tendencies in the world would also change. As a man changes his own nature, so does the attitude of the world change towards him. This is the divine mystery supreme. A wonderful thing it is and the source of our happiness. We need not wait to see what others do."[40]

These words are often simplified into a quote attributed to Gandhi—"Be the change you wish to see in the world"— although the words in his autobiography seem to be his closest to that now-famous quote. Their deeper meaning is illustrated by a legendary story often attributed to Gandhi.

A mother once came to him, worried about her son's sweet tooth. She asked Gandhi to tell her son to eat less sugar. Gandhi sent her away and asked her to return in 15 days. When she returned, he told the son to give up sugar. Why did he wait for so long before speaking these simple words? Gandhi said he first had to give it up himself before he could tell another to do the same. The deepest example of this wisdom in Gandhi was the concept of nonviolence. To gain the strength to practice true nonviolence in the face of British imperialism, he knew that he first had to bring the principle into his life, his mind, and, most important, his inner being. Gandhi taught truths by living them. He led from within.

The greatest trailblazers and innovators in history had the courage to think differently, even in the face of naysayers and skeptics who doubted or even dismissed their ideas. Most revolutionary change agents bring a 3D perspective to an existing, seemingly insurmountable challenge. While insiders sit paralyzed by fear or analysis, they power ahead undaunted. By the time others realize what has happened, such leaders have taken the problem and its solution to a new level. They gain followers because of what they believe and what they stand for.

Our actions in the world are a reflection of our thoughts. When the two are aligned, we get the highest expressions of our humanity. When they are not, we often live with a feeling of unease, one that can be suppressed but not surmounted until we face our true selves.

As a society, we are hungry for leaders who stand for their convictions, come what may—those who fight for what is right. Sometimes we see "leaders" in positions of great power, prestige, and privilege—which they worked a lifetime to attain—toss it away in a flicker of a moment when led astray by the weaknesses of their 1D or 2D mind, leading to ethical or moral transgressions.

Living our truths in the world is not a skill to learn but wisdom to remember. In business school, I took an entrepreneurship class that was taught through case studies of mistakes and failures. In each class, the subjects of that week's case study visited to share their lessons learned. I realized that the most authentic entrepreneurs were unafraid to face challenges because they were unafraid to face themselves. Not that doing so was any easier for them. Many of them had overcome devastating personal and professional crises before attaining their ultimate success. Rather than having less to face, most had more. Yet they embodied confidence, trust, and respect. They knew which values they stood for, which principles they lived by, and why.

Our values are the foundation for our authentic voice and guide us through the storms and fog of life. They anchor us and are the foundation of true leadership—in our own lives and in the world. In a data-saturated world, it is more critical than ever that we gather our own wisdom, formulate our own thoughts, and contribute our authentic voice.

Then we can push our boundaries more confidently, knowing that where life will take us is guided by our inner voice. This is the secret of true success. Each one of us is an inventor, an entrepreneur, and an innovator, born with a unique voice. It sings with joy and whimpers with sorrow but can, when carried with integrity through our days, like the great voices of ancient times, sway the foundations of humankind.

CHAPTER FIFTEEN

New Journeys

> You are here to enrich the world, and you
> impoverish yourself if you forget the errand.
> —Woodrow Wilson

The power of ideas—ones that can save lives, change minds, or elevate society—has defined the very trajectory of humanity. We have built civilizations, formed philosophies and religions, invented tools of progress, and created art and music, all beginning with simple thoughts. While physical relics, such as cities and artifacts, crumble with the ages and their creators rarely outlive a century, ideas survive. The words of philosophers, poets, scientists, and sages course through our neurons with the same intensity as they did through their authors' millennia ago. By contemplating them, we keep their eternal fires burning.

The true power of an idea rests in the minds it reaches. When an idea enters many minds, each mind can take it to a new place. This is the way society transforms—a person at a time, a generation at a time, a civilization at a time.

Even though the world population has exploded from less than 1 billion at the turn of the 19th century to more than 7 billion today, individual voices, ideas, and thoughts can now be disseminated faster than ever. For instance, assume that you send out an electronic message to two people at 1:00 p.m. and that each person who receives it transmits it to just two new people (who have not yet received it). Assume such a transmission occurs every 15 seconds and, hypothetically, that all humans are plugged into the same electronic grid. At 1:00:00 p.m., two people have received your message. At 1:00:15 p.m., four people will have received it from them. At this rate, by 1:08:00 p.m. the entire world population will have received it—just eight minutes later!

Even though it is available to us on a less perfect and efficient scale, the speed of transmission in our times creates incredible possibilities. Technology presents us with the opportunity to live out the global sense of interconnectedness that ancient civilizations imagined in much more philosophical terms.

At the same time, it is ever more important, in our modern technology-driven world, to also remember the philosophical wisdom of interconnectedness that has traced its way through most of our faiths and cultures over the centuries. While ancient societies did not live in a digitally connected world, many lived by timeless holistic perspectives on interconnectedness.

Many Native American cultures held a reverence and closeness to nature that nurtured harmony in their interactions with it. They had a long-term perspective and viewed natural resources as the precious lifeblood of the earth—as integral parts of a holistic, connected ecosystem—not as commodities for thoughtless human consumption. Many spiritual and cultural traditions, shaped by centuries of human happiness and suffering, also teach the same fundamental principle that we are all connected and that our deepest truths are eternal and unchanging.

I first experienced such a sense of interconnectedness when I stood in that schoolyard in Finland, on my first day at Malms Skola. I realized that an Indian girl born in Germany could connect at the level of the heart with Finnish schoolchildren who at first were wary of her different looks but soon realized she was not that different. We formed bonds that transcended any of the definitions the adults in our world might have created about who we were or how we should see ourselves.

I had the same feeling when I stood on that MIT street corner on a winter afternoon. I realized that all human cells speak a universal language. One that is oblivious to the differences our words delineate between us. Today, physicists recognize such unity at the most fundamental level of our building blocks. The world's atoms and molecules are held together by bonds, which are energy fields. Some bonds are irreversibly formed and others remain in perpetual formation and disintegration. Through their intersecting atomic orbitals we are all connected.

I also sensed deep interconnectedness that dawn during my yoga teacher-training program in California. That morning, sitting in stillness, I realized that, beyond the feelings of our hearts, and the movements of our cells and atoms, we are all the same at a deeper level—that of our inner energy. And our connection at that level exists within each of us and between all of us.

In all three instances, spanning three decades of my life, I experienced the 3D mind. When we look at the world through it—whether at the level of hearts, atoms, or beings—an incredible sense of unity emerges, one that transcends our known ways of knowing ourselves.

~

The mind and the universe are equally mysterious. Each encompasses an infinity that we can sense but not completely grasp. Looking at the night sky, when we see stars flickering in the distance, we realize that our seemingly vast and varied Earth is just a tiny speck. And each one of us is just a fleeting visitor on it—a single drop among billions in humanity's ocean through time. Superficial differences, alternate ideologies, individual likes and dislikes appear silly in the face of the recognition that, in its purest essence, all matter is composed of the same basic building blocks and all humans carry the same source of energy within them.

This perspective leads to a more holistic view of the world. How can we think of water as a commodity when we realize that the same water that we drink today once thundered through a river, supported a whale, and rained gently on a flower bud? Each time we turn on the faucet we are using a precious resource. Realizing that life depends on it, how can we waste it?

Such a mindset leads us to building a more sustainable world. Sustainability is based on the aspiration to have greater harmony or alignment with nature—a desire for an existence that is meaningful and restores the earth and is not defined by shortsighted transactions with nature and each other. Such thinking extends to the way we eat, the way we live, and the way we make our daily decisions. It brings more compassion into our hearts and more love into the world. It leads us to solutions focused both on our individual good and on the greater good.

The wisdom of the 3D mind leads us to do only good in the world because it reflects the essence of potential goodness that resides within each of us. Why do we seek to have a positive impact on the world? It is because impact gives us meaning larger than our selves and our lives. The feeling of being one person and helping to improve the lives of many others gives us a sense of connection and allows us to embody interconnectedness. Then we live the most universal human mission: to advance all of us. We begin to see the possible in the impossible.

It is as if we rediscover that the earth is round—not in a literal sense, but at a deeper level. We recognize that no matter which way we walk, our paths lead back to where we began. We are the ones transformed along the way. Life is not about destinations, because the world is a sphere, and each time we arrive, we continue on a new adventure.

We live in the best of times for realizing human potential and are fortunate to have communication tools that make sharing and spreading ideas easier than ever. We can transform our world starting where we are, with what we have. What we need today, more than any resource or skill, is this foundation of progress for invention and reinvention and disruption and reconstruction. This extends from our careers to our economies, from our health to our societies, and from our selves to our world. When we understand the wisdom that we are all connected, we create new paths—

ones we wish to walk *and* ones that pave the way to a better future for generations yet to come. Once we realize that our potential is boundless, why limit our lives? We need dreams that are bigger than the boundaries of our thoughts, and solutions that exceed the depths of our challenges. The power to reinvent the world and the first step toward making it possible always starts with an individual—it starts with you.

And One Last Thing

Not all those who wander are lost.
—J. R. R. Tolkien

The inner journey is the work of a lifetime. Its metrics of progress exist in no measurable dimensions. They are in our mind. To live our best possible life, we need to find our best possible path. It is easier to walk well-trodden roads. Yet sometimes it takes little extra effort to discover new ones. As wanderers and explorers have said through the millennia, if we keep going, the path reveals itself. Our true signposts are within. Outer signposts are there to help us get back on track. Once clarity emerges inside us, it guides our steps in the world. Then we just need the courage to follow them.

When you have a choice between taking the straight highway that looks far into the horizon or taking a diversion onto a small side path, it is much easier to do the former. This is especially true when almost everyone you know is on the main road. The scrubby side path is rarely straight.

It is filled with obstacles of all sizes that beckon you to quit at every turn. Few have walked it, so usually it has no signposts. Just as you think you have cleared one hurdle, another appears around the corner.

When you haven't gone too far, you can still hear others beckoning you to join them on the highway. They may be puzzled why you want to face risk and uncertainty when civilization has already built incredible roads. Some may question your judgment, shake their heads, and suggest you are lost and confused. You might even get pity and friendly, unsolicited advice on how to find your way back to the road, or even offers of free rides.

You might try to explain that what you see beyond the horizon is not visible from the road, although sometimes it is easier not to even try. Simply remember, each time you are questioned you are given a chance to retest the strength of your convictions and to look more closely at your map. Our inner compass gets us to our destination. Always. With each study of your paths, the journey becomes easier. Just remember, U-turns are possible more often than we have the courage to take them, and sometimes the most interesting parts of a journey are its detours.

For most of us, life is truly lived when we travel the raw, untrodden paths. In those moments, we discover meaning and feel most alive. Many highways lead to destinations that lose their luster when reached. We travel unaware, in a hurry to arrive, only to realize we forgot to stop and ask why we are on *this* road to pursue *this* destination. Fear leads us on some paths, the ego on others. Yet the secret is to pursue paths with wisdom. We complete many inner journeys alongside our outer ones, and although the world often doesn't see them, they shape who we become. Immersed in the craft of writing over the past two years, I realized that a book enables such an adventure—both for the one who carefully assembles the words and for the one who absorbs them. So I will leave you with a writing analogy.

Many of us live our lives in perpetual "draft" mode. We keep making edits, improving this, tweaking that, until we have the perfect masterpiece. Then we plan to finally hit the "print" button on our lives and present our best version to the world. Yet our life is a book that gets published each moment, each hour, each day. Each day becomes a printed page. We may change our perception of it, but the page has been printed. So, the only choice we have is to put our best words on the page. Our best words are not the longest or most complicated ones that showcase our mastery of vocabulary. The best words we can offer our life and the world are ones that emerge from our authentic voice. That way, rather than getting distracted by the mechanics of words, or of life, we can live their meaning.

As any writer knows, such words come to us in moments of grace. All we have to do is start "writing" the truths of our hearts into the world every moment—thought by thought, word by word, and act by act. Within those truths rest answers to the deepest questions we ask ourselves, each other, and the world. In them is the meaning of life.

Although we do not know when and where the stories of our lives will end, we can each ensure that when they do, we have a happy ending and a story worth retelling. Life is too precious and powerful not to do something that shakes the world a little.

Acknowledgments

My gratitude for this reaches back thousands of years to those sages who glimpsed humanity's essence in a form so pure their wisdom continues to reverberate through our neurons. Although I knew it to be true, writing this showed me once more that journeys truly are the destinations. For every step I have traveled, especially for all the detours, diversions, and unexpected U-turns—of which there have been many—I am grateful.

On every adventure, we meet new souls. Some become enduring bonds, while others may cross our path just once yet leave an eternal imprint on our heart. To all those I have ever met, on this and all the other journeys of my life, I am indebted. I am especially thankful to those who challenged me, disagreed with me, and saw life differently than I did—you led me to places I would never have arrived at on my own. I also owe an eternal debt to Harvard and Stanford. Both were much more than learning stops on my life's journey. Their professors—scholars, philosophers, and scientists, living and no more—generously shared their secrets for traveling well. They taught me how to become a student of life. Friends make our world, and family defines us. Words do not suffice, however eloquently laid out, to convey the depth of gratitude I owe to both in shaping my life—and these pages. When the going became tough, the road seemed too long, and the desire to quit loomed, you always suddenly appeared as if you knew—with the support, kindness, and love that, step by step, made a long journey possible. I am blessed for your being. While the heart is vast enough to contain all gratitude, the page runs out of space, so I'll mention here just those who most directly touched this—patiently reading and rereading these words and enriching them with their thoughtfulness. In no particular order, thank you to:

Mr. Rohde, for being my teacher, mentor, and friend. John Steinbeck once said, "I have come to believe that a great teacher is a great artist and that there are as few as there are any other great artists. It [teaching] might even be the greatest of the arts since the medium is the human mind and spirit." Mr. Rohde, your being a great artist changed my life. Your thoughts on these words did the same. Lynn, for reading an early draft with the wisdom of a professor, the encouragement of a friend, and the honesty of a coach—I cherished your sincerity and support every step of the way.

Rachel, for bringing—from the depth of our friendship—your honesty and wit; for challenging me, and for asking questions that always made me think. Jen, for bringing the perspective that only a college roommate can provide, especially since the years keep adding heft to it. Alice, for being a kindred spirit—your cheerfulness and our conversations always enrich me and had the same effect on this book. To Tony, for being you: in one word—awesome. You read this as if it were your own creation and extended your ever-warm hand to transforming its words and their author. To Ashish, for bringing your sincerity and thoughtfulness—a brilliant writer is hidden somewhere within you. To Divya, for the irreplaceable love of a childhood friendship that, rekindled after decades, feels as if it never missed a beat. Alan, I will always cherish our *Crimson* days, where I first learned the power of written words. For the honesty you brought to these, I am thankful beyond measure—you shifted my mind. Meena Aunty, you brought the loving warmth of an aunt and the sharp wits of an English professor to move this along—I am truly thankful. Finally, to Sunny—it takes a rare friendship to be a mirror that elevates our strengths and helps us overcome our weaknesses. For that, this book and I thank you.

I am also very grateful to Anne Dubuisson for your thoughtful insights on these words, and to Amy Fass, Drew Wheeler, and Annie Tucker for bringing the skill of your craft to bear on them. The Bethesda Writer's Center and my local independent bookstore, Politics & Prose, continue to nurture our community of writers and readers—they are local treasures. Many others guided this work in their own ways. My family across India and in Finland and England, your love keeps me connected to my roots. I often wish the continents were less vast—your being far leaves part of me scattered around the world. Donna, your courage humbles me—keep your beautiful light shining. Ehsan, Eric, and Jon, I can see clearly now—for memories that can still make me laugh, I am grateful. Terri, if the world needs more cheerleaders it should just clone you. Nandini, you inspire me—having you in my life is a true gift. And Kavita, for our unbreakable, enduring bond of sisterhood, which has enriched us both, I feel blessed.

And I leave the most difficult thank-you for last because, truly, there is no way ever to fully thank our parents. What you do for us emerges from a reservoir of love and generosity as vast as the universe. Mom and Dad, ever patient and ever encouraging—you not only taught me about human potential, you helped me discover mine. I don't know how I can ever thank you for that. I am trying to pay it forward—that's why I wrote this. Your love is in every word.

Notes

Chapter 1

1 "National Health Expenditure Projections 2013–2023," US Centers for Medicare & Medicaid Services, http://www.cms.gov.

2 "Chronic Disease Prevention and Health Promotion," Centers for Disease Control and Prevention (CDC), http://www.cdc.gov/chronicdisease.

3 "Health & Education: Any Mental Illness (AMI) among Adults," US National Institutes of Health (NIH), National Institute of Mental Health (NIMH), http://www.nimh.nih.gov.

4 "Medicine Use and Shifting Costs of Healthcare: A Review of the Use of Medicines in the US in 2013," IMS Institute for Healthcare Informatics, http://www.imshealth.com.

5 "Depression Fact sheet, October 2012," World Health Organization (WHO) Media centre, http://www.who.int/mediacentre/factsheets/fs369/en.

6 B. W. Stewart and C. P. Wild, "World Cancer Report 2014," WHO, International Agency for Research on Cancer, 2014.

Chapter 2

7 "Global Status Report on Alcohol and Health 2014," WHO, http://www.who.int/substance_abuse/publications/global_alcohol_report/en.

8 "A Pocket Guide for Alcohol Screening and Brief Intervention," National Institute on Alcohol Abuse and Alcoholism (NIAAA), http://www.niaaa.nih.gov/publications/Practitioner/pocketguide/pocket_guide.htm.

9 "Fact Sheets–Alcohol Use and Your Health," CDC, http://www.cdc.gov/alcohol/fact-sheets/alcohol-use.htm.

10 T. J. Kaptchuk et al., "Placebos Without Deception: A Randomized Controlled Trial in Irritable Bowel Syndrome," *PLoS One* 5, no. 12 (2010): e15591.

11 Tenzin Gyatso, "Our Faith in Science," *New York Times*, November 12, 2005.

12 Ibid.

13 Ibid.

14 "Complementary, Alternative, or Integrative Health: What's In a Name?" NIH, National Center for Complementary and Alternative Medicine (NCCAM), http://www.nccam.nih.gov/health/whatiscam.

Chapter 4

15 "Leading Causes of Death," CDC, National Center for Health Statistics, http://www.cdc.gov/nchs/fastats/leading-causes-of-death.htm.

16 "Injury Prevention & Control: Adverse Child Experiences (ACE) Study," CDC, http://www.cdc.gov/violenceprevention/acestudy.

Chapter 6

17 J. Stachel, "Einstein and Michelson – the Context of Discovery and the Context of Justification," *Astronomische Nachrichten* 303, no. 1 (1982): 47–53.

18 C. R. Thien, ed., "Illusions Can Survive With Science Says Maurois In Pegram Manuscript," Brookhaven National Laboratory *Bulletin Board* 22, no. 20 (May 16, 1968): 1.

19 Friedrich Kerst, ed., *Beethoven: The Man and the Artist, As Revealed in His Own Words*, trans. H. E. Krehbiel (New York: B. W. Huebsch, 1905).

20 M. K. Gandhi, "Speech at Meeting of Missionaries," chap. 139 in *The Collected Works of Mahatma Gandhi* (electronic book), vol. 32 (New Delhi: Publications Division Government of India, 1999).

Chapter 7

21 "Wisdom and Healing," panel discussions with military veterans moderated by congressman Tim Ryan, Wisdom 2.0 Conference, San Francisco, CA, February 2013.

Chapter 8

22 "The US Weight Loss Market: 2014 Status Report & Forecast," Marketdata Enterprises Inc., http://www.marketresearch.com.

23 Hunter Willis, "A Personal Story," *Washington Post* Live 2013 Childhood Obesity Summit, Washington, DC, September 27, 2013.

24 American Academy of Sleep Medicine, Standards of Practice Committee, "Best Practice Guide for the Treatment of Nightmare Disorder in Adults," *Journal of Clinical Sleep Medicine* 6, no. 4 (2010): 389–401.

25 Ibid.

Chapter 9

26 Edward W. Desmond, "Interview with Mother Teresa: A Pencil in the Hand of God," *Time*, December 4, 1989.

27 H. A. Jack, ed., *The Gandhi Reader: A Sourcebook of His Life and Writings* (New York: Grove Press, 1956).

28 Rainer Maria Rilke, *Letters to a Young Poet*, trans. Stephen Mitchell (New York: The Modern Library, 1984).

29 Ibid.

30 Ibid.

31 Charity Tilleman-Dick, TEDxMidAtlantic, Washington, DC, October 2012.

Chapter 10

32 Joseph Gaer, *The Wisdom of the Living Religions* (New York: Dodd, Mead & Co., 1956).

Chapter 12

33 M. K. Gandhi, *An Autobiography: The Story of My Experiments with Truth* (Boston: Beacon Press, 1993).

Chapter 13

34 Henry David Thoreau, *Walden* (New York: Thomas Y. Crowell & Co., 1910).

35 Ibid.

36 Henry David Thoreau, *Class Book, 1837–1900* (Cambridge, MA: Harvard University Archives, 1780–present).

37 Samuel A. Jones, ed., *Bibliography of Henry David Thoreau with an Outline of His Life* (New York: De Vinne Press, 1894).

38 Bradford Torrey, ed., "October 28, 1953," in *The Writings of Henry David Thoreau: March 5–November 30, 1853* (Boston: Houghton Mifflin Co., 1906).

39 Ibid.

Chapter 14

40 M. K. Gandhi, "General Knowledge About Health," chap. 153 in *The Collected Works of Mahatma Gandhi* (electronic book), vol. 13 (New Delhi: Publications Division Government of India, 1999).

(Please note: All website links are current as of August 2014.)